CW01551483

TALES OF A GANGES BLOATER

H.A. Smith

MINERVA P

LONDC

ATLANTA MONT

TALES OF A GANGES BLOATER
Copyright © H.A. Smith 1998

ISBN 1 86106 921 9

First Published 1998 by
MINERVA PRESS
195 Knightsbridge
London SW7 1RE

Printed in Great Britain for Minerva Press

TALES OF A GANGES BLOATER

Preface

The author hopes the title will set you thinking. What does it mean? The name is derived from HMS *Ganges*, Shotley, Ipswich, Suffolk; it was the toughest Naval training establishment in the world. The author joined the Royal Navy there as a boy of fifteen years in 1936 for a period of twelve years' service from age eighteen. At HMS *Ganges* he served a total of four years, one year as a trainee and later three years as an instructor.

He saw service at sea for all of World War II in many war zones and battles. In 1950 he was due to join the police force but could not do so because of the Korean War, and served in the Royal Navy until 1952, leaving HMS *Ganges*, Shotley as a chief petty officer. Without a break in service he then joined the old West Suffolk Police Force, serving until October 1978 before retiring as an inspector. (His total unbroken service was forty-two years and three months.)

The stories are all true and are mostly his personal experiences in the Royal Navy and the police service.

The 'Bloater' in the title of the book is derived from the fact that the author is a native of Great Yarmouth, Norfolk, famous for its cured herrings of that name. All native Yarmouth people are nicknamed 'Bloaters'. His family are all seafarers, his grandfather and father were drowned at sea (grandfather 1906 and father 1941).

The author hopes you enjoy reading the book as much as he enjoyed writing it.

Contents

Bruno RN

THE YEAR was 1919; the First World War was over, but the Revolution in Russia necessitated the despatch of a number of British warships to the Baltic to look after British interests.

Among them was one of our C-class light cruisers, HMS *Curacao*, a smart little ship built under the Emergency War Programme in 1916. These ships were some four thousand five hundred tons and at this time mounted single six-inch BL guns. (They were by World War II very efficient AA cruisers, having been converted.) One day HMS *Curacao* lay off a Russian port, a small place where there was absolutely nothing to interest the crew; there was no television or radio, no films or similar entertainments in those days, and the men had to make their own pastimes.

Four or five of the crew obtained permission to go ashore on a hunting expedition, taking with them .303 service rifles. The hills and woods around the town presented the promise of a pleasant ramble, and it was more of a lark than a hunting expedition; a day out, something different to break the monotony of a life at sea.

As they blundered through the thick undergrowth they did not really expect to see any wild animals, let alone have the opportunity to kill any. Suddenly and quite unexpectedly, the party found themselves confronted by a huge wild bear, which reared up and roared as it saw them approaching. Seeing it apparently preparing to attack, the sailors got rather excited, brought their rifles up to their shoulders and fired; the bear fell dead.

Collecting their rather shaken wits, the sailors walked over to examine the body. They were standing around the big bear when, to their surprise, they heard a loud whimpering. Next moment, a small bear cub came out of the undergrowth, walked over to the body and tried without success to wake his mum.

Sailors are soft-hearted men, and the sight of the cub nuzzling the mother bear and the sound of its mourning squeals made them feel awful. The mother, they realised, had only been trying to protect her cub when she reared up at them, and any satisfaction they had felt at their hunting prowess evaporated as suddenly as the bear had appeared in front of them.

What were they to do? They looked at the orphan cub, and decided that he did not stand much chance in Bolshevik Russia, apart, perhaps, from the chance of becoming the ingredients of a bear pie for the local inhabitants. There was, they decided, only one thing to do, take him back to the ship with them.

That was what they did. Their appearance with a bear cub aroused some consternation on board, but after the situation had been explained, the captain and senior officers agreed that he should become the ship's mascot. And so it was that the little bear waxed fat, his fur became sleek and shiny, and over the following year he grew very large on his diet of Tate and Lyle treacle on bread, honey when it was available, and loads of other titbits forced on him by the ship's company.

As he grew bigger, 'Bruno', as the men named him, became rather more playful. On several occasions he blotted his copybook as far as the sailors were concerned, by his antics, and there were some who felt their mascot was outgrowing his welcome.

About a year after the bear had joined the ship's company HMS *Curacao* was on a courtesy visit to a Turkish Black Sea port, Constantinople (now Istanbul), and tied up alongside a Turkish cruiser. Despite the fact that Britain and Turkey had been on opposite sides in the First World War, and that the Turks had given us a drubbing at the Dardanelles, relations were very friendly and everyone got on very well together. Bruno joined in the friendly exchanges, and the Turkish sailors took a shine to him.

When the time came for HMS *Curacao* to leave, it was decided to give Bruno to the Turkish cruiser as a farewell gift. It was a gesture of goodwill that did not please Bruno.

As the British cruiser left port, Bruno could be seen on the upper deck of the Turkish ship, playing up hell. Nobody could hold him, he was so big and strong, and so angry at losing his pals on the *Curacao*. There were some long faces on His Majesty's ship, because not everyone had wanted to give him to the Turks.

The months went by, and sometimes sailors wondered what had become of their old mascot. A year or fifteen months later, the British cruiser paid a return visit to that same Turkish port, and as they entered, the sailors saw that the Turkish cruiser to which they had given Bruno was lying in the harbour. When they were still more than a mile away they saw a huge splash alongside her, and as they steamed towards the Turkish vessel they could see someone, or something, apparently swimming towards them.

Somebody got his binoculars on the swimmer.

'Bloody hell! It's Bruno!'

The ship stopped so that the bear could be winched on board.

Bruno was very excited to see some of his old pals, but he was very thin, his once-lovely coat looked like a moth-eaten carpet; the British sailors were appalled at his appearance. The bear was given a bath, his coat was brushed, and he was fed his favourite treacle and honey sandwiches, and a tot of rum. Before long, he had settled down, and the Turkish sailors were told he was staying on board his old ship. They were not bothered in the least.

The British cruiser returned from her cruise to England. On the way, Bruno waxed sleek and fat. He was a much changed character, more obedient, caring, but he still had a bit of the old devil in him to cause an uproar if he could. He never got nasty, just pretended to be to get his own way. (Would you like to argue with a 500/600 lb. bear pretending to be nasty?)

He used to sit by the ship's rum tub on the ship's deck when the daily rum ration was issued at 11 a.m. each day (on the dot). He would sit there watching the different mess representatives getting their mess rations, not batting an eyelid. The older members of the supply branch staff responsible for dishing out the rum would make sure that, even adding water, there was a ration for Bruno this was all the stuff left in the tub. Rules and regulations decreed that all residue in the tub was put down the scuppers (drains). This would be supervised by the ship's 'Officer of the Day'. One day, a new store supply assistant dished out rum rations, supervised by a newly arrived Officer of the Day. When all rations had been issued, the new stores man, in accordance with the rules, tipped the residue down the nearest drain. Bruno, sitting quietly nearby, awaiting his perks, got a bit 'niggly', he rushed forward, picked up the stores assistant with his mighty front paws and began squeezing him, roaring his head off. One of the older sailors nearby told the Officer of the Day near the rum tub, what was wrong.

He said, 'Go and fetch some rum, sir, from the store, water it, and bring it back quickly for Bruno. I will talk to him till you get back.' The officer dashed away to get the rum. Bruno got quieter as his 'friend' consoled him but he would not let go of the unfortunate stores assistant until the officer arrived with his rum ration. The stores assistant had to be sedated and funnily enough he never tipped 'Bruno's ration' down the drain again. Nor did anybody else. After his ration, and his dinner, Bruno made friends with the stores assistant he had almost squeezed to death as if to say 'I did not really mean it.'

All men, on joining the cruiser *Curacao*, had to be paraded before Bruno and sniffed by him all over. Woe betide anybody walking round the ship that he had not sniffed. He got most uptight and angry, all visitors had to go through the sniffing routine unless they wanted 500 lb. of angry bear on their rear end in a hurry. The upshot of this was that when the cruiser came home to the Naval Dockyard she was due for a refit. She was hauled into dock on arrival there at about midday. Bruno had had his daily rum ration, his dinner, and in true Naval fashion, went to sleep in his den about 2 p.m. His den was a large circular gun support complete with door, full of blankets, toys, bits and pieces that Bruno liked.

During the first hour of siesta, about one hundred dockyard workers, technicians and engineers came on board the ship, complete with toolboxes, coats, cushions, kneelers and tea flasks. (Bruno was very 'niggly' if he had his siesta disturbed.) About 3 p.m. a dockyard worker started hammering loudly on the outside of Bruno's den with a large hammer, fitting a piece of equipment. This woke him up. He pushed open the door of his den, and to the horrified amazement of the dockyard workers this huge Russian bear emerged from the gun support, beating his chest and roaring over the fact that they had not been sniffed plus they had disturbed his sleep.

Mayhem ensued, some one hundred dockyard workers already on the ship, with their toolboxes and equipment, etc., which had taken over an hour to get on board, all tried to leave the ship at once, down two narrow gangways, as an enraged Russian bear, beating its chest and roaring, ran round the upper deck. Some jumped into the dock, some threw their gear over the side before jumping themselves and the scene was chaotic. (Somebody had forgotten to tell Bruno they were coming.) It was a good job the dock was still flooded.

Bruno stayed on the ship providing laughter, interest, and a diversion from everyday routine. He never harmed a thing. His appearance was terrifying but he was a gentle giant as soft as soap.

About 1925/26 Bruno was still ship's mascot. The British cruiser was on a visit to Greece and the Greek Islands. One day, a party of sailors from the ship decided to take Bruno ashore in a fairly rural area and let him have a 'roll and a run in the grass' after being cooped up on the ship. They were ashore, Bruno was running and rolling in the green vegetation and having a whale of a time. Suddenly he saw some sheep and goats in the distance. He ambled towards them as he always played with hairy animals. He thought, More fun. However the elderly Greek shepherd/goat herder who was nearby, grabbed a huge old-fashioned blunderbuss rifle, waited till Bruno was at point-blank range and shot him dead, despite yells from the sailors of 'No. Please don't shoot.' The sailors buried him where he fell with tear-filled eyes and with borrowed tools. The Greek shepherd was very fortunate he was not put in the grave with Bruno; at first the sailors felt like shooting him with his own blunderbuss but soon realised he was only protecting his flock.

HMS *Blean*

About 1943, the North African invasion by the Allies was going according to plan. The old destroyer I was serving on was in Algiers harbour (HMS *Wishart* built 1916). We had been a maid of all work with coastal convoys to supply the British 1st Army along the North African Coast, heading towards Cape Bon to join the famous 8th Army (Desert Rats) pushing on from El Alamein, to Cape Bon. We were ordered to escort a convoy of many old empty well-known troopships from Algiers (ex luxury liners) through the Straits of Gibraltar, and on its way to England.

We left Algiers with some twenty old liner troopships in convoy. All were destined for further troop-carrying work round the world. The Royal Navy escorts formed up around the convoy as they left Algiers harbour *en route* for England. We, the convoy, sailed towards Gibraltar and arrived off Oran, the famous former French port. We saw a new, fast, small British destroyer coming out of Oran Harbour to join the convoy escort, the *Blean*. (All named after famous fox hunts in England.) She joined the escort and was signalled by the senior officer of the escort to take station on the outside starboard screen of the convoy, the most exposed vulnerable position of the Naval escort, to combat a submarine attack on this valuable convoy.

The *Blean* took up her station next to the old destroyer I was on about a quarter of a mile away, on our starboard beam. This was all routine stuff we had endured on hundreds of convoys, we did not pay much attention. At 4 p.m. on the day in question, I took over on the duty gun. As captain of gun I checked all the crew were present, the gun and ammunition were all correct, and performed any other chores. All was in order. It was a beautiful Mediterranean day, no wind, sunny, blue sky, and the duty cook appeared on our deck with the tea. We all got our cups, and began to enjoy it. Not a care in the world despite the war; we sunned ourselves on deck.

Suddenly at about 4.50 p.m., I heard a violent explosion on the starboard side towards the *Blean*. I looked in that direction and saw a white plume of water shooting skywards level with the *Blean's* funnel (the only one). I knew she had been hit in a vulnerable point by a torpedo (I had seen too many). Within seconds there was a similar explosion and, on looking at her again, I saw a second torpedo had hit her under her stern, propellers and rudder area, a plume of water shooting skywards. (A nine hundred and fifty ton small destroyer, two torpedo hits in under a minute, and she had disappeared under the waves.) My watch registered fifty-eight seconds from the time the first torpedo hit until she vanished beneath the waves, after the second torpedo hit her.

My destroyer turned out of line and headed towards the area where the stricken vessel had gone down. Another destroyer nearby circled us as we stopped to pick up survivors of the *Blean*, with her asdics going, to try to prevent another submarine attack on us, whilst picking up survivors. We knew that, despite the law of the sea regarding saving human life, the Germans would ignore it and sink us if they got half a chance.

With this in mind, we set about picking up survivors, the sea was thick with black oil fuel from the *Blean's* newly filled oil tank. Our rope nets from the upper deck to the sea were full of sailors from the *Blean*, climbing up to safety. We were rather hesitant in all we did in case another well-aimed enemy torpedo committed us to the deep. All the survivors were covered in thick black oil fuel, and were hard to help as they were so slippery, but we did our best.

I was tending the scrambling nets on the bows of the ship, yelling orders at the survivors as to what to do and above all 'to get a bloody move on' before the submarine that got them, which was somewhere nearby, did the same to us.

One young lad in the water called up to me, 'I cannot climb, my leg is done for.'

I threw him a rope and said, 'Put that under your arms, and tie a bowline knot at the front, we will pull you up.'

He caught the rope in the water, tied it to himself as instructed and with two or three helpers we pulled him on board. On deck he stood on one leg, dangling the other. I saw one of his feet pointing to the front of him, the other foot was pointing in the other direction, directly behind him. I realised he had a badly broken leg.

I said to him, 'How did you get that?'

He replied, 'I sat on deck reading a book, near the stern, there was a bloody great bang as the torpedo hit us. I looked up in the air and coming down on the top of my injured leg, from a great height, was one of our own 300 lb. depth charges, evidently blown off the stern by the second torpedo.'

We picked him up and carried him to shelter, laid him down, gave him a shot of morphine and left him, to go and assist other survivors. As I got to the scrambling nets again there was a large 'able seaman' trying to climb the net. He was some six feet tall and about fifteen stone. He was complaining loudly about back pains. We, my destroyer, had been stopped for some time and we were not sure if we were next in line for a 'tin fish' from the enemy sub. I yelled at him to get up the net fast, we helped him with a rope round his shoulders and at last he reached the guard rails round the upper deck and stood outside them.

I said to him, 'Come on, old cock, get over the guard rails on to the deck.' I put my hand round the back of his neck and pulled him towards me. The guard rails were level with his hips, and I bent him over the rails till he toppled over the top rail on to the ship's upper deck. He was about the last survivor on that part of the ship. He was still complaining about his back pain. We gave him a shot of morphine, marked his forehead in indelible pencil with time of dose and the date, to stop any other eager beaver coming along after we had left and giving him another shot. Two or three of us carried this large lad and laid him full length on deck under cover of the ship's bridge etc. and hurried off to assist with more survivors being pulled on board up the rescue nets further along the ship.

I was helping on the lower part of the upper deck of my destroyer, pulling in oil-soaked survivors, when one 'body' we had pulled in looked at me and said, 'Hello, you young bugger – how are you getting on?' I looked at the oil-covered body and wondered, 'Who the hell is this?' He looked at my petty officer badges and said, 'You seem to be doing all right for yourself.' He raised an oil-laden arm and hand, wiped his face and hair as best he could and I saw he was a leading seaman (corporal) who had served with me in the Navy from 1937 to 1940; he had been one of my instructors under training as a boy seaman in 1937. He was still a leading seaman. I now outranked him. This made no difference.

I said, 'Hello, Ginger, you old bugger, come with me.' I took him on one side, all survivors had been rescued and we were on our way to rejoin the convoy.

Just before I found Ginger I had helped to pull two oil-soaked gentlemen in RAF uniform up the rescue nets. Both wore RAF pilot's wings, medals and sergeant's insignia of the Royal Air Force. I said to the first one we got on board, 'RAF? What the hell were you doing on the *Blean* when she was sunk?'

He said, 'We were ferry pilots from Gibraltar to Oran, we flew Spitfires assembled from crates in Gibraltar to Oran airfield. We were on passage back to Gibraltar to collect some more aircraft. I sat on deck reading a book, it was warm and sunny, we were enjoying it, not a care in the world when there was this f— great bang. The next thing I knew I was flying through the air and landed in all this oily water, we didn't see anything, we didn't hear anything, and suddenly we were nearly drowning. We were both Battle of Britain pilots and if this is what the Navy has to put up with, you can stuff it. I am not getting on another one of these [warships] in a hurry. I would sooner take my chance in a dogfight at four hundred miles-per-hour in the sky with enemy planes – at least you can see the bastards coming, with this lot you don't stand a chance.'

I said, 'How many RAF lads were in your party?'

He replied, 'Four of us.'

I said, 'I am afraid you are the only two left, I have seen most of the survivors and you are the only two left.'

He said something like 'Bloody hell,' and I left them.

I went back to where I had left Ginger, I took him to a quiet area in the ship's boiler room, on top of the boiler, got him two buckets of hot water, a towel, some of my own vests and pants, socks, shirts, etc. and left him to clean himself up. The Royal Navy in wartime did not make any provision for re-kitting of survivors, all clothes meted out to survivors came from the kit of the rescue ship's crew, to replace it, they then had to buy new kit out of their own pocket, money which was never reimbursed. How could you stand by and see oil-soaked survivors of ships at their wits' end after getting rid of oil-soaked gear, with no clothes to put on to replace their useless clothing? We all looked after them, supplying our own gear, and buying more when we could afford it.

When I went back to Ginger he was cleaned up, dressed in my clean undies and boiler suit. He said to me, 'That is better, there is only one thing I need now to put me right.'

I butted in and said, 'Yes, I know from the old days, you want a couple of tots of Pussers rum.'

As I said this I pulled my bottle of illegal supply of rum out of my pocket and his eyes lit up, he grabbed the bottle, downed about a quarter of a pint, laid down, gave me the near empty bottle and said, 'You are a pal.'

I left him to sleep.

As I left Ginger I went up on deck to find the ship was doing a speed of some thirty knots to catch up with the convoy we had left. I looked at the confusion on the upper deck as we tended survivors, gave first aid to the injured etc. and thought, What a mess. We had rescued eighty eight men from the *Blean* of her total complement of one hundred and eighty eight men, including RAF and other passengers. I was thinking of the carnage when I suddenly thought, What has happened to poor old matey?, the big fellow we had pulled up out of the water, complaining of back pains, who we had sedated with morphine and laid on the deck under the bridge structure. Had he been seen to by others during the operation, or was he still there, with the ship going hell for leather to catch up with the convoy, and half a gale roaring past?

I ran up on to the fo'c'sle to where we had put the big lad complaining of his back, and to my consternation he was still there. I ran up to him, knelt down beside him spoke to him without result, shook him, and no response. I felt his pulse and realised he was dead.

I hurried from the scene to find the ship's doctor, who had his hands somewhat full with some sixty to seventy casualties in amongst the *Blean* survivors. I found him, told him the story and we hurried back to where I had left the back-injured lad dead.

On arrival, the doctor, a lieutenant, gave the body a cursory examination and then said to me, 'Give me a hand to turn him over.'

We both, working together, turned the lad over and the doctor ran his hands down his back on the spine.

After his check he looked at me and said, 'His spine is shattered in two places, I am not surprised he is dead.'

I looked at the doctor and said, 'When we hauled him up on the scrambling nets, I got hold of him round his neck and pulled him on board over the guard rails, bending him in the middle as he came on board, could this have killed him?'

The doctor replied, 'I doubt it, the injuries to his back were fatal, and if it is any consolation to you, if he had survived he would have been a helpless wheelchair-bound invalid for the rest of his life, he wouldn't have wanted that.'

The doctor left to go about his duties tending the injured and wounded. I went back to where I had left the other young lad we had pulled on board whose feet were pointing in opposite directions.

When I arrived I said to him, 'How are you now?'

He looked at me and said, 'Not very sharp. My leg is hurting like hell.'

I looked at it and the top of his leg and thigh looked like a pig's back, his trousers were skintight around the leg. I said, 'Your leg wants attention, are you okay otherwise?'

He replied, 'No I have been given a few tots of rum by your helpers. It was very nice but I now can't pee.'

He had a bucket alongside his bunk and I said, 'Can you do anything now?'

He replied, 'No I am bursting for "a strain of my cabbages" and cannot go.'

Once again I dashed off to find 'my friend' the ship's doctor, who said, when I found him 'What the hell is wrong now?'

I explained the problem to him, and he said, 'This lad cannot pee, he has a broken leg or thigh, and I suppose you and your bloody cohorts have been giving him rum.'

I said, 'Well I suppose so.'

He shrugged and said, 'If this lad has a double rupture you lot have not been doing him any favours by stuffing him with rum. Come on, let's go and see what we can do for him.'

On arrival in the compartment, the doctor had a quick look at the patient and said, 'I thought so, a double rupture.'

The lad lay on the bunk, clutching his stomach with tears in his eyes saying, 'I can't pee.'

The doctor opened his little black bag and came out with a glass tube, this he wielded towards the lad's nether regions. He then got hold of the boy's penis, inserted the glass tube down the end of it and kept pushing it up inside him, at the same time shouting, 'Bucket.'

I grabbed a bucket nearby and the doctor told me to hold it under the end of the glass tube inside the lad's penis. Suddenly urine started to run down the tube into the bucket I was holding and the injured lad let out groans of delight such as 'Ooh', 'Ahh', 'Lovely' etc. as his bladder was emptied. On completion the doctor said, 'He is to be given no more liquid of any kind until he has been to hospital, and treated.'

I replied, 'Yes, sir.'

The Surgeon Lieutenant then said to me, 'Right we have dealt with that problem, now let us have a look at his damaged leg and thigh.'

The lad lay on the bunk, his injured leg flopped sideways, his foot outwards. The leg, badly swollen, made his bell-bottom trousers tight from below his knee to his crotch.

The doctor said to me, 'Right, cut his trousers off so I can get at that leg.' I whipped out my Bowie-type sheath knife I always carried at sea. I got hold of the bottom of his trouser leg, put my knife inside and, with one stroke cut his trouser leg from the bottom to above the crotch. The doctor shouted at me, 'Be careful with that bloody knife, I only want his trousers off, you nearly castrated him.'

He examined the badly swollen leg and said it had two bad breaks above the knee at the thigh, and one just below the knee. He told the lad he would set the leg as best he could and splint it till he got to hospital in Gibraltar.

The doctor made me sit down near the head of the injured lad and said to him, 'Put your arms around the petty officer's neck and when I pull and adjust your leg, if it hurts, squeeze his neck, as if you are strangling him, you don't get a chance like this every day.' Smiling at him he said, 'Are you ready?'

The lad said, 'Yes.'

The doctor pulled on the injured leg and turned it, the lad groaned and squeezed my neck. My face went blue and my tongue swelled under the pressure, I thought I would pass out. Then the lad let go and I flopped back nearly suffocated. The doctor said to me, 'That is one break now we will do the other.'

I said, 'Hang on, sir, I haven't got my wind back yet.'

He replied, 'You have got the easy bit, he has got the pain.' He said to the lad, 'Right, same again.' The lad put his arms round my neck, the doctor pulled, twisted, held the injured leg. The patient squeezed my neck, nearly choking me, yelling in pain. The doctor finished his temporary setting of the leg. I laid back like a half-strangled haddock, rubbing my neck and throat, trying to breathe again. The doctor splinted the leg said, 'Well done all,' grinning at me. Then he picked up his little black bag and left to deal with other dead and wounded.

The convoy was approaching the Straits of Gibraltar, three or four columns of the majestic old ladies, all famous names. We could see the Rock, with Spain behind it, and Morocco on the left. We rubbed our hands at the thought of docking in Gibraltar, landing the dead and wounded for the hospital, then getting a run ashore after weeks at sea, to drown our sorrows. Our anticipation was short-lived. We were suddenly ordered to turn the convoy round on an opposite course, away from Gibraltar, and steam at fast speed in that direction. We could not understand this so I sought out my fellow NCOs in the signals department to find out what was going on. I was told there was another large convoy of troopships in the Straits of Gibraltar, fully loaded, heading for the war zone. We had to get out of the way to allow them to clear the Straits and avoid two large convoys meeting head on in the rather narrow Straits.

This was no major setback except, with the large number of wounded on board requiring urgent hospital treatment, it was no joke. At last we turned and headed back towards the Straits and *en route* passed the other convoy we had avoided in the Straits, now in the open Mediterranean Sea. As we approached Gibraltar we knew our convoy of empty troopers were bound for Blighty. We expected to drop off near Gibraltar and land our sick and wounded.

As we drew level with Gibraltar our captain made a signal to Admiral in command Gibraltar requesting permission to detach from convoy (leaving them to other Royal Navy escorts) to enter harbour and land casualties from the *Blean*. The reply really made us wonder what was going on. The reply was, 'You will remain with the convoy until you are relieved.'

We passed through the Straits of Gibraltar, passing Cape Spartel and Cape Trafalgar as we entered the Atlantic Ocean and turned towards the United Kingdom. The ship's doctor was dealing with casualties he really did not have facilities for in an old destroyer, overcrowded enough before we picked up eighty eight survivors of the *Blean*.

Some thirty miles out in the Atlantic we received a signal to detach from the convoy and return to Gibraltar some seventy–eighty miles away. The captain really hammered the old ship back to harbour. We were met by ambulances, doctors, nurses, etc. which could have been available two or three hours earlier. No doubt the Admiral had a good reason for his actions, which we did not know about, and never did find out.

I said goodbye on the gangway to my old shipmate Ginger, he was sober by then having drunk my rum, and walked ashore in my kit. I never saw him again from that day to this.

The lad with the pee problem and the badly broken leg, I said goodbye to as he was stretchered to an ambulance from the gangway of our ship, on his way to hospital. Some two years after the end of the war I was attending the Royal Naval Hospital at Gillingham, Kent, from the Royal Naval Barracks at Chatham, Kent, with some medical complaint. I was in petty officer's uniform, walking along the street, still a serving regular. I heard a shout from across the street, looked in the direction of the noise and saw a young man in civilian clothing waving. I thought, Who the hell is he? I don't know anybody from this neck of the woods. Another loud shout, the person across the road was waving. I crossed the road and saw this young man, complete with a 6 to 8-inch tall soled surgical boot, leaning on a stick.

I said to him, 'Are you calling me?'

He said, 'Yes, don't you remember me?'

I said, 'No I am afraid I don't.'

He replied, 'You were a petty officer on the *Wishart* in the Med during the war and you picked up the survivors of the *Blean* – I then recognised him as the "non pee merchant" and remembered his broken leg. I shook hands with him, we had a chat and he thanked me for what I had done for him and apologised again for nearly strangling me when his leg was set. He was out of the Navy and had been for several years because of his leg which, after several operations, mended some six to eight inches short, hence his surgical boot.

Another curious sequel to this story occurred about six months after the war ended when I was in a pub, on leave, in my home town and a chap approached me and shook hands. Despite his facial scars I recognised him as an old Navy friend, a regular like me, who had been badly wounded on his destroyer at the evacuation of Dunkirk. His wounds and blindness in one eye meant he was invalided out of the Royal Navy in about 1941. I asked after him and his family, whom I had known for years. He told me his family was okay except for his mother. I asked what was wrong. He explained that his younger brother, also an RN man, had been lost with his ship in the Med about 1943. His mother had received the telegram from the Admiralty that he was missing presumed killed when his ship was lost, but would not accept the fact that the boy was dead; he was her favourite son. She had it in her mind he had been picked up and was somewhere suffering from loss of memory and that he would eventually return home. He added that this state of mind is 'driving her nuts'. He said that they had been in touch with the Admiralty and all sorts of people and could not find out anything as to what happened to his ship. I sympathised with him and his story and then said to him, 'What ship was your brother on?'

To my surprise he said, 'HMS *Blean*, a Hunt Class destroyer.'

You could have knocked me down with a feather. I said to him, 'I was on the ship next to the *Blean* when she was sunk and I was one of the NCOs who compiled the list of survivors. I can tell you now your brother did not survive, he went down with his ship. If you have got time I will tell you what happened.'

He said, 'Have I, fire away.'

I told him the story as outlined here and at the finish he shook hands warmly and said, 'Now we know it's coming from you, Mum will now accept my brother is dead, she will be much better.' He left the pub to go to tell the story to his mum.

Another queer twist to the story, whether true or not, is that the *Blean's* anti-submarine detector gear was not working properly when she joined the convoy off Oran. The young captain, afraid to 'lose face' on being newly promoted to a command of his own ship, failed to inform the senior officer of the RN escort of this fact, and he was therefore assigned to the most vulnerable position on the outside of the anti-submarine RN ship screen, with disastrous results. (This was revealed by some of the survivors we spoke to from the *Blean* after rescue.)

Medals

It was the Queen's coronation year. I was a not-so-young police constable, having completed long service of sixteen years in the Royal Navy including World War II and the Korean War. I was now serving in a rural Suffolk market town. It was 2 a.m. in the police divisional headquarters which was no Waldorf Astoria for eating in. We, the assembled audience in the canteen, about five-six officers, were nearly all ex-servicemen. The twelve foot by eight foot room with an ancient gas cooker in the corner and a couple of tables and four or five chairs was the canteen. There were a few utensils like a kettle, teapot, frying pan and a slice (to retrieve bacon and eggs from the pan if you had any, these were the luxuries). All cooking, making tea from your own supply, etc. was up to you.

When you arrived at the station about 1–2 a.m. to feed, you had forty-five minutes to cook, make tea, change or dry wet clothes, eat and get out again on patrol. Needless to say, night duty grub was a flask of tea and sandwiches, you then just got time for other natural functions if you were lucky.

During the refreshment break, we were all munching sandwiches, drinking flasks of tea and talking together when one of the senior constables present, an ex-guardsman of the Grenadiers, said to the assembled audience, 'I have been selected to attend the coronation by the chief constable, to line the streets of London during the function. I have got to wear my best uniform and medals. Force orders state that if your medals are a bit ropy you must put in a written report with your medals, requesting that they be re-slung etc. My medals are not so good and I have to send them in to be re-slung but how on earth do I word the report to the superintendent to get them done?' (He was never very good at his paperwork and sometimes required help from other officers.)

An old Army man in the room winked at the rest of us, when 'somebody' was looking the other way, drinking tea and eating. He said to the questioner, 'How tall are you?'

The ex-Guardsman replied that he was six feet one and a half inches.

The questioner said, 'Well that is easy, just submit a report to the superintendent requesting that your medals be re-slung for coronation duty to fit a man six feet one and a half inches tall.'

There was a silence in the room. All eyes swung to the ex-guardsman, some almost gurgling with suppressed laughter. He said, 'What the b— hell has my height got to do with my medal ribbons?'

The old Army wag said, 'A lot, when you get to London for the coronation parade, the officer in charge will fall all the policemen in, in a straight line for inspection. He will say, 'tallest men on the right, shortest on the left.' He will then go to the end of the rank and look along the uniforms of the men in the rank to see they are all in a straight line. He will also look at the silver of the medals on display on the men's chests which must be in a dead straight line. The tallest men on the right must have long medal ribbons about eight to nine inches long. The ribbons of the others along the ranks vary in length to the shorter men on the extreme left with medal ribbons some three to four inches long. This is so all the medals hang in a dead straight line when the reviewing officer checks them. So you see, the height of the men on parade is essential for medals.'

The old ex-guardsman said in his Cockney accent, 'I didn't bleeding well know about that.'

The leg puller said, 'You live and learn.'

The old guardsman left the canteen to type his short report and submit his medals. (No typists in those days.)

Some four days later I was back on day duty, assisting the station inspector to reorganise his court work, due to new legislation. I was happily checking new forms in his office, glad of a rest from pounding the pavements, when there was a muffled roar from the superintendent's office next door and he burst through the door waving a report form.

He said to the inspector, 'What the hell is this report all about? It is from PC — stating he has to go on coronation duty, requesting that his medals be re-slung to fit a man six feet one and a half inches tall, what the hell is the matter with this man?'

The superintendent, himself a World War I veteran, was very irate. The inspector was nonplussed and the superintendent said him, 'Your bloody signature is on this report, why the hell didn't you pick it up?' The inspector was speechless, I was nearly killing myself with laughter nearby and the superintendent said to me, 'You are laughing, you know what is going on in this station, tell me the story.'

Controlling my mirth as best I could, I told the full story to him. At first he was rather angry but at the finish he couldn't stop laughing and returned to his office in tears. He came out a short while later gave me the ex-guardsman's report and said, 'Rehash this and sign it "p.p."

for him and re-submit it to me.' I did this and no more was heard by me or the dear old ex-guardsman. He went to London on duty and had the time of his life complete with new medal ribbons.

Rural Detectives

The year was about 1946/47, near Christmas time in a Suffolk Village nigh unto a very large United States Air Force base.

Food was still partly rationed but it was always available if you had the money and knew the right people. One of the local constabulary sergeants, of great experience in the Army and the police, was on duty in the local police station with one of the constables in the evening, when a smallholder came in who lived on the outskirts of the village and reported that he had had some seventy five plump cockerels stolen which he had been bringing up for Christmas money. He explained that he bought them as day-old chicks, earlier in the year, had fed and watered them for about nine months and now some so-and-so had stolen all of them from a large shed on his smallholding, just prior to Christmas.

The sergeant logged all the details, and told the complainant he would do his best to find the missing livestock. (Probably now dead stock.) When the despondent smallholder left the station, the sergeant said to his constable friend, 'This job has all the hallmarks of Mr — and his son.' These men were also smallholders, who lived about a mile from the aggrieved person. He added, 'Unless you catch them with the goods in their hands, they will not even tell you the time.' He added,

'Softly, softly, catchee monkey, play this lot with care.' He then said to the constable, 'Mr — and his son usually go to the local pub about 8 p.m. and stay there drinking until chucking-out time. We will wait till they have gone to the pub and then pay a visit to the house whilst Mrs — is there.' This good lady was as hardened a criminal as her son and husband and they couldn't expect a lot of help from her.

The sergeant, with his colleague, went to the house and the smallholding of the suspects at about 9 p.m. He walked up the garden path to the house past some chicken huts. He told his colleague to wait whilst he opened the door of the chicken hut, put his hand inside, felt around and then, with a pull and a jerk, his hand came out with a handful of chicken feathers, which he thrust into his police overcoat pocket, still clutched in his hand. He knocked on the door of the house, the lady came to the door and immediately shouted, 'What the hell do you want?'

The sergeant stepped into the door, all seventeen stone of him and said, 'We are investigating the theft of seventy-five chickens from Mr — up the road, we think your husband and son may be able to help with our enquiries, where are they?'

She replied, 'Up the pub, we don't know anything about stolen chickens so you lot can p— off.'

The sergeant said, 'You know nothing of any stolen chickens?'

She said, 'No.'

He said, 'You have had no chickens on these premises at all?'

She replied, 'No, we do not know anything about any chickens.'

The old sergeant then reached down under the kitchen table, with his fist full of the chicken feathers he had snatched from the chicken hut in the yard on his way in, pretended to grope under the table and then stood up straight, opened his hand, which was full of chicken feathers, and said to the woman, 'Where in your kitchen do these come from when you know nothing of any chickens?'

She stared wide-eyed at the feathers in the sergeant's hand and shrugged her shoulders in defeat. She said, 'Before they went to the pub I told those two silly buggers to clean up all the feathers after they had killed and plucked the chickens in here. Look at what they have left behind,' indicating to the sergeant's hand.

He then said, 'Where are the birds now?'

She said, 'In the shed down the garden.'

They went there and recovered seventy-five freshly killed and plucked cockerels and removed them to the police station.

The next move was to go to the local pub and arrest the culprits celebrating their latest acquisition. Father and son were removed to the police station protesting their innocence until they were shown the chickens and then they were completely gobsmacked. (Another crime detected.)

Royal Navy Unskilled Medical Diagnosis

The year was 1949, about January/February, I was serving in a large Home Fleet Battle Class destroyer. I was a Senior Petty Officer and the ship's gunnery instructor (Master Gunner). We were lying in Chatham Dockyard, our home base. In the chief and petty officers' mess I was Mess President, a post very reluctantly accepted by me. I was elected against my real wishes, but by general consensus of the sixteen members of the mess. They persuaded me to accept the office. I knew this lot in the mess were bolshie, uncooperative, and downright obstructive to anything that happened to alter their daily routine or upset them. Most were World War II veterans, they knew all the answers, and most only had a short time to serve before finishing their time, and couldn't care less.

Our dear old messman, a senior able seaman, who bought, collected, and prepared our food in the mess, was demobbed. I was the ship's organiser and regulator. I put several young men in the job but they were all a calamity. Most of them, who had all served in big ships, where all food was found, cooked, provided, ready to eat, were no expert male Fanny Craddocks. They could not make pastry, prepare stews, make gravy, make desserts, dumplings, and buy all the ingredients. The moans from the mess members at me went on and on. (I am fairly thick-skinned but doing my normal gunnery job and trying to pander to all their moans and groans I was sorely tempted to tell them to stuff the job of Mess President and let them sort it out.)

I was standing on the upper deck of the boat in Chatham Dockyard one morning when I saw an able seaman pushing a handcart along the dockside towards our gangway, with his kitbag and hammock thereon. By his badges on his tunic sleeve I gathered he was a regular Royal Navy man, some twenty six or twenty seven years of age (easy, he had two red stripes like a corporal on his arm, and you only get the second stripe at twenty six years of age or thereabouts).

He stopped his handcart at the bottom of our gangway, I thought he might be going past, and with a bundle of papers in his hand came on board. He saw me and came over. He said, 'I have been drafted to this ship – can I report to you and give you my papers?'

I said, 'Certainly.' Looking at this fresh-faced young man I immediately thought of my problems in the mess on the ship. I said to him, 'Have you served in small ships before?'

He replied, 'Yes.'

I said to him, 'What are you like at cooking? Say knocking up clacker.' (Royal Naval name for pastry, dough, puddings.)

He replied, 'All right. I have done it all before.'

I thought this is the answer to my prayers. I said, 'How would you like to take over as chief and petty officers' messman?' (A cushy job usually with certain privileges.)

He said, 'Suits me.'

I said, 'The job is yours.'

I went below to tell the then messman he could have a change of job and he almost wept with relief as he did not like all the flak he got from the chief and petty officers for his culinary efforts. He was gone in no time and the new man moved in.

It worked like a charm, this new fellow was a bit of an expert at cooking. All the food was good, well-prepared and cooked. The moaning minnies in the mess could find no fault, and life resumed on a more even keel. (I thought, I am on a winner here.) The mess bills for food were kept down, we all had plenty to eat and we were reasonably happy. No blots on the horizon.

After about ten days to a fortnight after the new man joined, we learned we were to be attached to a task force bound for the Arctic Ocean. Our job was to test all new equipment, clothing, ship's gear such as guns, torpedoes, time worked on deck, amount of food needed and smaller ship's oiling at sea from tankers and aircraft carriers, by different methods, in case we went to war with Russia.

All men were issued with some four sets of clothing, all men had to eat four special meals a day, extra doctors were taken on board, we had four instead of one, and lots of other gear for additional tests on guns, torpedoes and toilets. These were peculiar on Russian wartime convoys to Archangel. At the start all warship toilets froze solid and were unusable in the far north. Buckets and hot water were pressed into service on all ships to relieve the natural functions of the crew. Result: near chaos – we were not prepared.

Some boffin then invented steam pipes to be put round the inside rim of the toilet pan which kept them frost-free but gave half the Navy piles.

We, the task force, sailed for the Arctic Ocean. The force consisted of an aircraft carrier, a cruiser, some three or four large destroyers, a submarine and a Fleet oil tanker. We went north with the task force up to Iceland, Bear Island, Spitzbergen, etc. We stayed up there for about three to four weeks, and despite the weather boffins on the expedition predicting where the rough, freezing, gale-force winds were, we were unable to really find what we wanted regarding really cold weather. At times it was warmer than the United Kingdom. However we soldiered on.

At one point we were practising oiling at sea, a gale was blowing, weather rough, heavy seas, and we went in for a practice run at the Fleet tanker. We came up astern of her, rolling and pitching. She was trailing white buoys astern, we had to come up astern of the tanker slowly, pick up the buoys with grappling hooks and haul up the tanker's oil pipe over our bow and connect it to our ship's fuelling system. Not an easy task in a near gale, on a heaving destroyer's deck. We carried out the move three or four times and were successful, but on the last run we rolled, swayed away from the tanker, strain came on the oil pipe and it burst. Stinking black oil fuel carried by wind, water and rain smothered the whole of the front of our destroyer and we looked like a huge chocolate destroyer, enveloped in smelly oil fuel. Gun turrets, bridge, mast, decks and anything else you can think of were all covered.

We cast off the tow and retired to lick our wounds – the mess was appalling on our usual clean spick-and-span vessel. We knew a hell of a lot of work with special oils, cotton waste, and elbow grease would be needed when we returned to base, to clean her up.

We recovered a bit from this little lot and carried on, with the task force looking for cold weather off Greenland without success to try to carry out our tests.

One day during this time, I walked to the stern of the ship along passageways to visit below-deck magazines and shell rooms, take temperatures, and see everything was in order in the ammunition department. As I approached the chief and petty officers' bathroom I heard running water and knew somebody was taking a shower. I went to check to see if some crafty b— in the crew was having a quiet illicit shower when nobody was about. I slid the bathroom door open and saw our prized messman/cook taking a shower. One of his perks of the job of messman to chief and petty officers' mess was to use our bathroom, a bit more civilised than the crew's.

He was drying himself on his towel as I entered the bathroom. He stood naked and I looked at his body which had drawn my attention despite seeing hundreds of naked bodies in the Navy as an NCO, instructor at training schools, etc. His torso was completely covered in small red-purple bumps which looked like boils, hundreds of them. They only showed below his shirt neck, none on his wrists and hands, and when fully clothed you could not see them as they were covered by his clothing.

I stepped into the bathroom and looked at his skin eruptions, which were most unusual. I said to him, 'What are all those bumps and boils on your body?'

He replied, 'I don't know. They have only erupted in the past few weeks.'

I looked closely at the eruptions on his body and said, 'I don't like the look of this lot.'

He replied, 'Nor do I.'

After a few minutes of looking at his skin eruptions I said to him, 'Have you ever had syphilis (VD) in your Naval Service?'

He replied, 'Yes, I was in Haslar Hospital in Portsmouth until a few months ago with it, but before I joined this ship I was discharged as cured.'

I said to him, 'I am not a doctor but I am afraid it appears to me you were not cured. Get your clothes on and come with me.'

This he did and followed me to the ship's sick bay. I there told him to sit down and wait. I went to the wardroom (officers' mess) to see the four doctors on board for this special voyage. All were experts in their own field: diet, cold, exposure, stress and strain, treatment of freezing cold victims etc. Only one of the four young Royal Navy doctors had any experience in VD treatment and diagnosis. (Not really needed in the frozen north.)

I got the four doctors together and told them the story in private. They all looked at me as if I was nuts.

One said to me, 'Have you seen the man, what do you think he has got?'

I replied, 'He, in my opinion, has got secondary syphilis.'

Their eyebrows went up and one said, 'Have you ever seen this condition before?'

I said, 'No.'

They were all relieved, smiled and said, 'Well how the hell have you recognised this?'

I said, 'Many years in the Navy, listening to the gory tales of old sailors on long night watches convinced me that this man has secondary syphilis in an advanced state.'

They then decided to view and examine the man. I brought them to the sick bay, told the messman to strip in front of the doctors and left. Some time after, I was called back into the sick bay by the doctors, and they admitted they were not sure what the man had, as only the VD doctor had seen a case of secondary syphilis before and he was not sure what it was.

Knowing the repercussions, the captain of the ship I was on was informed, and the aircraft carrier's admiral was also informed. He ordered us to transfer the man in question to the aircraft carrier, which had a miniature hospital etc. on board and could treat the man in question. We closed with the carrier and transferred him by breeches-buoy with all his kit.

Once again we were minus a messman and my loving messmates were on the moan again regarding their grub, the lack of organisation, and how I had picked this fellow for a messman with suspected VD. We would all be contaminated.

The following day we received a signal from the Admiral in command on the aircraft carrier to the effect that the messman had got secondary syphilis and would be detained on the carrier in the sick bay till we got home in about a week. I informed the mess of the signal and all hell was let loose verbally. (It was my fault that the man had been appointed to the messman's job with VD, he had been going to the toilet and then mixing our food up and dishing it out, what was I going to do if all the mess, or most got VD from the food?) I tired of this talk, I knew the chance of catching syphilis from food etc. was very remote but I wanted action.

I went to see the doctors and explained my position, they were sympathetic and when I suggested a blood test for all in the chief and petty officers' mess as soon as possible, they agreed. Test tubes were prepared and labelled, and I was told to get all sixteen members of the mess to the sick bay by 2 p.m. that day, for a Wasserman test.

I had press-ganged a new reluctant hero to be messman, and after lunch all the chief and petty officers were talking, smoking, having a nap. I made sure they were all there, and about 1.46 p.m. I banged loudly on the mess table and in a loud clear voice I ordered them all to fall in outside the sick bay at once for a blood test. They were not very happy, some tried to argue but I silenced them by saying, 'This is an order, lawfully given, you know the penalty for direct disobedience of orders, now get up to the sick bay.' I made sure they all were there, grumbling like hell. I went in first and had my index finger wound with rubber tubing and stabbed with a needle, the blood put in a test tube and labelled. I then made sure they all got done and nobody dodged the test.

After we were all done, we closed near the carrier, rigged breeches-buoy, and transferred the tray of test tubes to her deck for test in her sick bay. After the test, which took the grumblers by surprise, there was an uncanny silence in the mess. They dared not complain for fear of another little surprise from me.

The next day we received a signal from the carrier which set out all the names of the blood donors and the fact that none of them showed any signs of VD. I took the sheet down to the mess and pinned it on the noticeboard and loudly told all the fainthearts that they were pure. After this they all stopped grumbling and in a few days we were bound for home.

As we arrived in the Thames Estuary on our way to Chatham Dockyard up the Medway River, we recorded the lowest temperature we had had for four weeks, even in the Arctic Circle looking for bad cold weather; it was ironic.

We surveyed our oil-laden destroyer, a dirty chocolate colour, and to our horror the next signal we received from the C in C Nore (Chatham area) was 'You have been selected as a ship to be visited by the public at the forthcoming Navy Week, please make all preparations for a good show.' Our captain told the C in C our predicament by signal with oil fuel on the superstructure, and we got a reply to the effect: 'In your preparation you will just have to work a bit harder.' We, the crew, worked all hours of the day and night for some four or five days to get the ship clean. We only just finished cleaning, scraping, painting etc. late on the day before we were open to the public. (Tired out all wondered why the hell we joined the Royal Navy.)

Russian Hospitality

The year was early 1949, I was serving in a Home Fleet battle class destroyer HMS *St Kitts*, all destroyers being named after famous British battles on land and sea. I was a chief petty officer. On the day in question I was duty NCO responsible, with the duty officer, for the efficient running of the ship. The ship was currently being re-fitted in Chatham Dockyard.

About 5 p.m. on the evening in question an able seaman ran along the upper deck to my office and said, 'Come quick Chief, there is a hell of a punch-up on the forward mess deck.'

I went to the scene straight away and on arrival on the 'miscellaneous branch' mess deck, used for cooks, signallers, writers, etc. I saw two rather 'groggy' young ship's cooks, who looked as if they had walked into a bus. One had a bruised nose streaming with blood, the other a nasty black eye forming, and both looked sorry for themselves. Standing nearby was a tall thin leading signalman, his eyes were rolling, he was white faced and shaking, he was extremely angry and he was threatening to continue the devastation by remarks like, 'I will knock seven bells of s— out of you two,' to the two young cooks.

I went up to him and gave him a direct order to leave the mess deck at once and wait for me in my office. At one stage I thought I was going to be assaulted but his wrath subsided and he left the scene. I looked around and on the bulkhead (wall) of the mess deck was a loudspeaker connected to the ship's radio system; the front was completely smashed and I could see the damage had been caused by a large electric iron, still in the ship's loudspeaker with the plug and lead hanging from the hole in the speaker.

I said to the two young ship's cooks, 'What the hell happened here?'

One of them said, 'The radio was on and it played the *Red Flag*, we were singing to it and giving the clenched fist salute, playing about, when the leading signalman went mad. He attacked me and my mate here, nearly knocking us out; we had been ironing our uniforms and he picked up the iron and hurled it at the loudspeaker, smashing it.'

I said to him, 'You know the rules about singing that song or any other Communist propaganda – it is a punishable offence on HM Ships; I will be back to see you two later, now clear up this mess and clean yourselves. Keep your mouths shut or you may both be in trouble.'

I left the mess deck and went to my office where the leading signalman was waiting for me to interview him.

I sat him down and said, 'What the devil came over you to hit those two junior ratings? As an NCO you could be in serious trouble for assaulting junior ratings.'

He replied, 'Those stupid young bastards were singing the *Red Flag* and they haven't got a f— clue what it is all about.'

He was again getting angry. I said to him, 'Look here, what are you getting all worked up about over this incident?'

He replied, 'You don't understand.'

I replied, 'Well if I don't you had better enlighten me as it may save you being put on a misconduct form for assault on junior ratings.'

He drew a deep breath and said, 'I am not supposed to tell anyone about this but I think I will have to.'

The next hour or more was a real eye-opener for me, I was spellbound.

He said, 'It is not long ago since I was released from a Russian concentration camp after three years inside and I had a gut full of them. Those two young bastards on the mess deck are lucky I did not kill them.'

I was taken aback at this and said, 'Tell me more.'

He went on to say, 'In 1944 to 45 I was stationed at the British RN Shore Signal Station in Archangel, Russia. Our job was to get our Russian Convoy ships into Archangel Harbour and tell them where to berth, refuel, get provisions, etc. after their trip from the United Kingdom; this was warships and merchantmen. We asked the Russians where they wanted them to berth etc. and we told the ships' captains in English, where to go, and what to do. I had been in Russia for some time. I met a lovely Russian girl whilst there and fell in love with her and we planned to marry and eventually come home to England after the war was over. One night in 1945, before the end of the war, I went ashore from the signal station, as I had done many times before to meet my girl at a rendezvous in Archangel, on "our street corner". As I approached our meeting place I saw two men run out of the shadows of the buildings and grab her by the arms. I was livid, I ran to help her and on getting there, I hit one of the men on the jaw with my fist and downed him, the other drew a baton out of his coat to hit me. I got it away from him and clouted him with it – he went down like a log and never moved. Suddenly they were joined by three or four more men. I downed another one but finally by weight of numbers I was forced into a vehicle and driven away to a lock-up. I do not know what happened to my girl after the punch-up. At the lock-up, in a large building in Archangel, nobody would or could talk to me when I tried to ask what was going on; I was slung in a cell for the night, and left.

'The next morning the cell door opened and in walked a pleasant-looking well-dressed young man who spoke English. He introduced himself as my Russian legal representative sent to assist me. His opening words were to the effect, "I am given to understand you have got yourself into a bit of trouble?"

'I replied, "I cannot see how I got into trouble when I went to the help of my Russian girlfriend who was being attacked at night, on the streets of Archangel by two strange men, I didn't know what they were up to."

'The Russian lawyer then said, "Those men you attacked were members of the official secret police. The girl you are friendly with is causing the authorities concern because of her close friendship with you, and they decided to break up your association with her and she was being officially removed for her own benefit."

'I said, "How was I to know they were members of the secret police? I thought when they grabbed my girl they were robbers, rapists, thugs, intending her harm. Surely you can understand this and explain things for me."

'The Russian lawyer said, "You have told me your side of the story, I will come to court with you this morning. We will see what can be done."

'After making notes in the cell, the Russian lawyer was called by the guards and I went off with him into another part of the building where we were ushered, or should I say shoved, into what appeared to be a court.

'On a raised platform in front of a gathered assembly were seated three severe-looking black-bearded gentlemen. I was told to stand up by my Russian lawyer "friend" whilst something was read out from the raised platform. I was then told to sit down. Another character got to his feet in front of the raised platform with the three black-bearded gentlemen thereon, who were listening intently to what he said. At times he pointed at me and everybody scowled in my direction including the three black-beards.

'I nudged my Russian lawyer friend two or three times during the proceedings and said, "What are they saying?"

'His reply each time was, "Keep quiet, you must not keep interrupting and talking."

'I then asked him when he was going to say something.

'He hushed me again to keep quiet.

'Finally the man who had been addressing the court and the black-bearded men on the raised platform sat down. I was told to stand up by my Russian lawyer. I did so and the centre one of the three black-beards on the platform glowered at me and said something in Russian to my lawyer friend alongside me, who made a very short reply, again in Russian. I said to him, "What did he say?"

'He replied, "You were just sentenced to three years in a Russian concentration camp."

'I said to him, "That is bloody marvellous. Why didn't you say something on my behalf?"

'He replied, "You must be joking, I do not want to finish up in the concentration camp with you."

'He then left. I was disgusted but could do nothing.

'I was bundled into a vehicle and removed to a Russian camp, near Archangel. The British Government, I understand, were not informed and as far as they were concerned I was posted as a deserter having defected to the Russians, when I failed to return to the signal station from shore leave when I should have done.

'In the camp I was stripped of my uniform and given some ill-fitting prison uniform to wear. I was forbidden to communicate with anyone except my fellow Russian prisoners; they could not speak English, I knew little or no Russian so I was not going to communicate with anyone.

'We were housed in bleak, cold, bare, barrack-type buildings, we were fed once a day on watery vegetable soup and a hunk of evil-tasting bread. All my fellow prisoners were political prisoners, I managed to find out. We worked hard all day, spurred on by clouts from the guards' rifle butts, fists or batons. Some or most of the guards were women – they were vicious bastards, worse than the men. They must have been hand picked.

'I lost track of time and a lot of weight, all I concentrated on was staying alive. I don't know if I imagined it or not but when the guards issued the soup and bread daily I seemed to get a little extra soup and bread, which kept me alive. A lot of the Russian prisoners died. This did not perturb the Russian guards – it was accepted as part of daily routine to dispose of dead Russian prisoners.

'Not long after I arrived in this first labour camp I noticed a rather "different" Russian prisoner among my fellow inmates. He was middle-aged, quiet and was more refined in his habits than the others. It took me some time to get to know or even approach him as he kept himself to himself. I gradually gained his confidence and found he could speak perfect English. He turned out to be a university professor and he "took me in hand" after he heard my story and got to trust me. He taught me to speak and write in Russian after a few months. He enjoyed teaching me on the few occasions we had the time. This made quite a difference to me when I knew what the guards, fellow prisoners etc. were talking about.

'I began to take interest in time and dates, and became more settled under very adverse conditions. I learned from my new-found friend, the college teacher, that he was in the camp because he had been teaching in classes in college one day when he passed rather derogatory remarks in his lecture about the Communist regime's latest Five Year Plan which was not working out, any more than their previous Five Year Plans. One of his students informed the secret police of "his teachings" and he was arrested, brought before a secret court and was sentenced to five years in the labour camp.

'During my three years in Russian camps I was moved three times to different camps, in different parts of Russia. There was no transport. The whole camp marched on foot, dozens of miles a day, in ice, snow, freezing winds, no warm clothes or footwear, no medical help whatsoever. Many died *en route* from natural causes, others by more violent means. A "lady guard" saw a Russian prisoner stagger out of the line of struggling marchers to try to grab a handful of grass showing through the snow, to eat as he was starving. He didn't make it. She shot him dead before he had taken three paces. "Trying to escape," she said. Hundreds of miles from anywhere, in snow, starving, ill, no equipment to use, or food; she must have been mad.'

He went on, 'After some three years of this in about 1948, I had lost all sense of time. I was ill, starving, half-dead, and I was half the weight I was when I was imprisoned. I was taken from the camp by truck, I don't know where, to a port of some sort in Russia. In the harbour was a British merchant ship. The Russian truck stopped at the ship's gangway, a Russian officer and soldiers dragged me, half-walking, up the gangway and threw me on the ship's deck to the amazement of the crew members. They were crowding round me, a dirty, thin, emaciated bundle of rags on the deck. The Russian officer bellowed to a ship's officer nearby, "This belongs to you." He then left the ship and the truck drove away.

'I was only semi-conscious when I heard the merchant ship's captain, who had prodded me, say, "Who are you?"

'I managed to croak, "Leading signalman —, Royal Navy, and my official number..." and passed out. When I next came to I was in a clean bunk, I had been washed, bathed and shaved and, I suspect, disinfected. A meal was awaiting with a drink which was most welcome. The ship's captain, when I was settled, took brief details from me and said he would inform his head office and the Admiralty of what had happened. After some time the captain came back to me and said, "I have to keep you under arrest, you are to be taken to London by this ship where you will be taken into custody by an Army escort who will be waiting. My next port of call should be Newcastle but this has been cancelled and you must instead be taken to London on suspicion of deserting to the Russians three years ago."'

He, the leading signalman, then said to me, 'I felt bloody awful but I could understand the dilemma the Admiralty was in. Here was I with my inside knowledge of Naval signalling and codes etc., friendly with a Russian girl, suddenly disappearing in Russia without a word from anybody. I thought to myself, I am in a right mess.'

He went on to say, 'About a week to ten days after we left Russia we arrived in the port of London. An army captain and six soldiers as escort came on the ship, arrested me and the officer gave the captain of the ship a receipt for "my body". I was taken to the truck and put in. I was then taken to a large building in London, locked in a secure room with an armed sentry on the door and told to wait. I had improved a bit in health on my voyage from Russia to London with rest and good food but I was still ill, underfed and grossly underweight.

'An Army doctor arrived and was let in by the armed sentry. He said to me, "I am going to examine you now. You will be kept here in custody. I do not know the details of what is happening but my concern is for your health. You are not in great shape as I can see and nobody will question you, visit you, or do anything without my consent."

'He then examined me for a long time and when he finished he said, "You seem to have 'weathered the storm' physically reasonably well but you must take it easy for some time." He asked for a rough outline of what had happened and I told him. He then went to leave and said, "Rest up, eat all you can but don't overdo it. You can order anything you like and you will get it. I will see you in a couple of days."

'He left, I was fed well, I had a bell to ring if I wanted things and I was treated well. After a couple of days the doctor returned examined me again and said, "Tomorrow, 'the powers that be' will start to interrogate you, I will be present at the interview and regulate the time of questioning. You will not be put under any strain for any length of time."

'The next day I was called up and fed, dressed, taken to a room in the building and told to enter with the doctor. In the room was a large horseshoe-shaped table with admirals, generals, air-marshals, and men in civilian clothing. I was told I was suspected of desertion and had to convince the interrogators that this was not so. The doctor briefly examined me and gave permission for the senior officers to start questioning. I sat alone in a chair facing them.

'One after the other they asked me various questions about my arrest in Archangel before I was taken to the labour camp. The questions were very searching, thorough, and all speech was typed and recorded by a typist. After about thirty minutes the doctor examined me briefly and told the senior officers, "That is all for today." I was returned to my secure room under guard, and left to read, listen to the radio etc. I was not allowed to write letters or get in touch with anybody. My next of kin were informed I was alive and in this country but that was all.

'Then followed a week of daily questions from the senior officers, in the same room. Each day, the question time was longer, the doctor allowing the length of question time. At the end of the week I was called into the room and a senior naval officer in front of the other officers said to me, "We are now satisfied that you did not defect to the Russians and we can now relax a bit. You will be allowed to write censored letters home and you can lead as normal a life as possible *but* you will be kept in custody here for the next six months. You will be questioned by Navy, Army and Air Force senior officers for two months each at a time, under medical supervision. You must understand that you have vital information that you have gathered in three years in Russian camps that must be recorded; you may not appreciate what you know now but you have unwittingly gathered it."'

The leading signalman went on to say he was kept in custody until he had been questioned by experts from the three services for two months each. The questions were too numerous and complicated to remember but they ranged from weather, to dates of bad and good weather in each camp. What time did it get dark, light, what was the length of darkness and daylight on certain dates? What food did you get, how much, when did ice and snow set in, in each camp? What were the guards' clothes, weapons, ammunition made of, how long did they stay on duty, what was in the ground in the camps, sand, rock, soil? What work did prisoners do and how long could they work for? The questions were interminable but quite understandable in this cold war period when we might have gone to war with Russia.

'At the end of my six-months-plus "stay" in London, I was released, sent home on long leave, paid my three and a half years' back pay, and this is my first ship since returning to normal duty. Now perhaps you understand why I got mad with those two stupid young buggers and hit them. I told them to pack it in when they were singing the *Red Flag* but they wouldn't.'

I told him to go about his duties. I spoke to the two young cooks – they did not want to complain as they would be in trouble. The leading signalman wanted it kept quiet as he had broken the rules as well.

I had the loudspeaker and the electric iron repaired by the appropriate department and because of the delicate background to this incident, I thought discretion was the better part of valour.

(At the end of my talk with the leading signalman I asked him if he had seen or heard of his girlfriend after his arrest by the secret police and he shook his head sadly and said, 'No, I didn't.')

Shark Fishing
(Royal Navy Style)

The year was 1939, about May or June. I was an eighteen-year-old seaman on a Royal Navy cruiser, *Ajax*, of the South America and West Indies Station in Kingston, Jamaica. The ship had just circumnavigated South America via various countries to the Falkland Islands. From there the captain wanted to avoid Cape Horn for various reasons and we passed through the Straits of Magellan into the Pacific Ocean and up the West Coast of South America to the Panama Canal. After passing through the Canal we arrived at Kingston, Jamaica, for a courtesy visit. (Our trip had lasted some nine months.)

On the day in question, the majority of the younger seamen like myself had been hard at work since 6 a.m. We had started at the crack of dawn on the ship's quarterdeck. This was on the stern of the ship above the officers' quarters, and was a sort of revered place as this was the portion of a ship where Admiral Lord Nelson fell at the Battle of Trafalgar in 1805. On boarding His Majesty's Ships via the quarterdeck, all officers and men had to salute the quarterdeck as they boarded the ship.

Our job at 6 a.m. on the quarterdeck was to prepare the wooden deck for an officers-at-home party that night, which included a dance. All the local society bigwigs and their ladies had been invited to attend. Our job was to prepare the deck and the surroundings for the function.

To prepare the deck it had to be holystoned. This consisted of flooding the wooden deck with salt water from hoses. The young seamen were formed into a line across the deck from port to starboard. Trouser legs had to be rolled up above the knees, shoes and socks removed. A wooden slab was a kneeler, also wetted. The duty NCO then threw sand over everything and told us to get down on our bare knees on the wooden kneelers – the sand bit into your kneecaps each time you moved. Before getting down on all fours you were issued with what looked like two flat yellow-grey house bricks called holystones or prayer books by the users. You then, on orders from the NCO, scrubbed the wet, sandy, wooden deck with the bricks. On contact with the decks the bricks gave off a sort of wet brick dust which was supposed to whiten the wooden deck. You held one in each hand and scrubbed the deck with both of them at the same time. When you had finished one length of deck you were turned about and did it again. This diabolical practice played hell with your knees and lower limbs with sand grinding into them. After two or three hours of this it was getting monotonous. (We were lucky at Jamaica where it was warm; this practice was also carried out on visits to Northern Scotland in winter, when there would be ice on the deck, and freezing water. I know because I had been doing this on other ships since I was a boy of sixteen years.)

About 6 p.m. that day in 1939, worn out and glad of a rest, my old shipmate and close friend, nicknamed Ringbolt, and I were sitting on deck in the evening sun reading library books. The ship's awnings were spread above the iron decks to try to reduce the temperature below decks which was a steady ninety degrees plus Fahrenheit.

The cooling system inside the ship was a joke – you just sat and sweated. If you sat on a wooden stool (the usual seating) and got up to go anywhere you left a puddle of sweat on the seat.

The officers-at-home party was in full swing, the deck dry with the sun, liberally sprinkled with French chalk and thus ideal as a dance floor. The Royal Marine band was playing the current popular dance music and the assembled officers, guests, ladies etc. were having a whale of a time with the Royal Marine stewards serving drinks as if there was no tomorrow. (Ringbolt and I broke all the rules by lifting the screens around the quarterdeck and having a 'Bo-peep'. The ladies' gowns were nice, as was all the finery, little did they know of the blood and sweat by the likes of me to prepare for their jollifications that evening.

I put my library book down and said to Ringbolt, 'This is not very exciting.'

He replied, 'What else can we do? We have no money. We cannot go ashore, what do you suggest?'

I looked over the ship's side and said to him, 'I reckon there are sharks down there,' pointing to the water.

He replied, 'So what?'

I replied (being a keen fisherman) 'Let us try to catch one.'

Ringbolt said, 'You must be barmy.'

I said, 'All right let us prove it one way or the other. You go down to the ship's store and get a shark hook on loan [carried on all HM Ships as stores]. I will go and see the ship's butcher for some bait.'

Ringbolt left to get the hook, I went to the butcher's store to see if I could cadge some bait.

In the store I saw the ship's Royal Marine butcher. I said to him, 'Have you got any rotten meat to spare? I want to go shark fishing.'

He thought it was a huge joke and laughed at my suggestion but pointed to the butcher's hooks along the wall of the store and said, 'Over there is a half-leg of pork which has gone off. I was going to dump it but you might as well do it for me.'

Being an ex-butcher myself, I grabbed the smelly top end of the back leg of pork off the hook and departed to meet Ringbolt on deck. He shortly appeared with the shark hook, looking a bit disgruntled. The hook consisted of some six feet of chain, to the end of which was fixed a steel hook with a large barb, and the bow was some seven inches across, like a butcher's meat hook with a barb on the point. A fearsome-looking weapon. Ringbolt said to me, 'Jack Dusty [Naval slang for stores assistant] is a happy sort of bastard today. When I asked for the loan of the shark hook he said to me, "If you lose that bugger you will be paying for it for the next of your twelve years' service."'

I said to him, 'Never mind, we are in business.' I went along the upper deck and found some rope about two inches in circumference and about 30 to 40 yards long. I thought, Just the job, and took it back to where I had left my friend. I took the hook from him and impaled the huge portion of the smelly leg of pork on it. I bore in mind Jack Dusty's warning of paying for the shark hook if it was lost and remembered that Ringbolt's pay and mine at this stage was 2/– per day (ten pence in new money).

As I tied the rope to the chain of the shark hook, instead of the usual round turn and two half hitches, I gave it a round turn and four half hitches.

I looked over the side, we were at a point in the middle of the ship. I hurled the steel hook, pork bait and rope over the side and let the rope out until about twelve feet from the end. I then tied the thick rope to an iron awning post nearby, which held up the ship's awning. Ringbolt and I then relaxed, sitting on the wooden deck of the ship reading our library books. (The most exciting thing we eighteen-year-olds could do.)

The evening was still, not a breath of wind, the sea round the ship was like a sheet of glass. After about a quarter of an hour, the ship's awning over our heads started to flap. I stopped reading and looked up. The canvas awning was flapping as if in the wind. I said to Ringbolt, 'What the hell is doing that, there is no wind?' I looked towards the steel post we had tied the shark rope to and it was waggling from side to side, causing the awning to flap. The shark rope was quivering like a violin string when we went to look, and the rope sticking out at a forty-five degree angle from the ship's side was going round in circles in the water.

I got hold of the rope and felt a great strain on it. I said to Ringbolt, standing alongside me, 'I don't know what we have hooked on here, but it is big and heavy.'

He said to me, 'You are pulling my leg.'

I said, 'All right, get hold of this rope and feel it.'

He did and said, 'What the hell is it?'

I said, 'How the devil do I know, we have got to pull it in to find out.'

The strain on the rope was so great I did not dare untie it from the awning post as I knew the two of us would never hold the thing on the end – it was too big. We called to various members of the crew nearby, who were relaxing and reading, talking, like we had been. I asked them to grab the rope and prepare to form up and pull like a tug of war team when I untied the rope from the awning post. When they were all ready I untied the rope from the post. It was ten men versus the thing on the other end and it was soon obvious we were not winning the tug of war, the thing was.

I went to a storage locker nearby and pulled out a large block and tackle which, if attached to the tug-of-war rope, in true Naval fashion, would increase the power of the pull. When I did this we were winning the tug of war and the thing was coming towards the ship. We hauled away until it was just below the water, alongside the ship. I looked over the side and saw it was a tiger shark some twelve to fifteen feet long with our shark hook in its jaws, biting on the chain to try to get away. It was a fearsome sight, its huge grey body and tail were thumping the ship's side making a booming noise, somebody said to me sarcastically, 'What is your next move?' The officers' dance went on and the band played only yards away.

My thoughts were, 'We have got to get the shark hook by hook or by crook, but how?' This shark was a monster and it was playing up hell, thrashing the water and the ship's side. I thought, 'We must kill it somehow. I suddenly remembered officers with sporting rifles. I told the lads to hang on where they were (not that they could do much else). I ran down to the paymaster sub lieutenant's cabin not far away. I knew he had a .22 sporting rifle (and was a nice chap). I arrived at his cabin, hammered on the door, and opened it virtually at the same time. He was lying on his bunk with a local young lady, fully clothed snogging and he said to me in the doorway, 'What do you want?' He spoke rather irritably (I wonder why).

I said, 'We have caught a tiger shark, sir, up on the starboard side near the torpedo tubes, it is playing up hell, could you bring your sporting rifle and shoot it for us, so we can get our shark hook back, if we can get it on board.'

He leapt up, grabbed his gun out of its storage locker and followed me up on deck. He went to the ship's side, looked over, saw the shark, leaned over, took aim and shot it expertly between the eyes. It gave a final lashing and lay still. The sub lieutenant then departed to carry on with his more interesting activities.

With the shark dead, we towed it along the ship's side until it was under our starboard torpedo davit (crane), which was used to lift torpedoes out of the water and back on deck after practice firing runs. We soon winched our catch out of the water, swung it on deck and laid it out in a clear space near a hosepipe and fire main. I cut the shark hook and chain from its large, gaping mouth, and said to Ringbolt, 'Take this back to Jack Dusty and cancel your loan of it in his book, we have been very lucky to get it back with this bloody thing.' Ringbolt shot off to get rid of it.

He returned and our party of some ten or twelve men looked at the huge corpse.

Somebody said, 'I wonder what's inside it, has it got any bits of bodies it has attacked and eaten whilst they were swimming from beaches round the coast?' (A daily occurrence.)

I said, 'Let us find out.' I nipped along the deck to see the Royal Marine butcher in his store and he loaned me a butcher's knife. I returned to the shark and said to the lads, 'Switch on the fire hoses and wash away the blood as I open him up.' The hoses were switched on, the water flowed freely and I opened up the dead shark's belly with the butcher's knife. Blood, intestines, bits and pieces went everywhere. We were completely oblivious to everything except the shark and my operation.

Suddenly our activities were interrupted by a yell nearby. I looked up and to my horror the ship's commander (second in line to the captain), was wading towards the shark party in his best uniform, shark's blood and guts over the top of his shoes, mixed with sea water. Absolutely livid, he shouted at me by name to stay where I was, followed by 'and the rest of you.' I glanced along the upper deck. In the activity, I had forgotten that the deck the shark was on was on the same level as that of the officers' dance. (The ship was designed so that, in battle, the wooden deck we were on when flooded with sea water would extinguish flaming shrapnel, and retain water for at least a depth of three inches). To my horror and consternation I looked beyond the irate Commander waving his telescope at me and saw officers and lady guests walking on tiptoe, holding up long dance dresses, wading through shark's blood, guts and sea water, with the Royal Marine dance band holding instruments aloft to avoid the water. It was total chaos, the dance deck was flooded, and the dance abandoned.

I had been on the commander's staff some six months before and I could not avoid identification. He yelled at me as he waded towards me, through blood and water in his lily-white suit, 'You go and fetch the master at arms, you are all on a charge.' I scuttled off and came back with the master at arms, the ship's policeman. At the scene of the disaster, the irate commander shouted at him (knee-deep in blood and guts) 'I want all these men on a discipline charge, and they are to come before me very shortly.' He was a very vindictive officer and we all knew we were for the high jump if we appeared before him after our shark fishing.

He stood glowering at us whilst the master at arms took our names, numbers, messes etc. to prepare his charge sheets for commanders defaulters (court). We were all apprehensive as we knew we could expect about fourteen days jankers (punishment) each.

Whilst this was going on I saw a lady of about sixty years of age wading through the blood and guts until she reached the commander's side. She arrived alongside him and he sprang to attention and saluted. I thought to myself, She must be one of the heavy mob to get this treatment. The good lady looked at our commander and said, 'Well done Commander. Did these men of yours catch this shark?' (She was standing over it.)

He, very embarrassed, replied, 'Yes ma'am.'

She said, 'Jolly good show, I hope you are going to encourage them to catch some more, these things have killed three people this week round the island. Well done.' The lady, who had been at the dance, then waded away. I then recognised her as the wife of a former Governor of the Island, who had died the year before. We had buried him at sea from our quarter-deck, she had been there.

Suddenly the commander seemed to mellow; he said to the master at arms, 'Tear up those lists of these men, forget any charges.' He turned to us and said, 'Throw that [the shark] over the side *now*! Clean up all this mess and clean the decks. I will inspect this area tomorrow.' We all turned to, cleaned the decks, the shark's blood, guts, etc., got rid of the body and heaved a sigh of relief to think we were not destined for fourteen days jankers thanks to the ex-Governor's wife.

Shipwreck

In late November, 1941, the escort group of corvettes my ship was attached to had just arrived in Gibraltar, after a fourteen-day trip from Liverpool, harassed most of the way by U-boats and long-range German bombers. Fortunately we had got our convoy of some thirty ships through to Gibraltar unscathed.

We had only been in Gibraltar some forty-eight hours when we received an emergency signal ordering us and every boat with asdics in Gibraltar, to sea. Some forty vessels were strung across the Straits of Gibraltar in two single lines. The first twenty or so vessels from Cape Spartel to Cape Trafalgar covered the entrance to the Straits of Gibraltar, from the Atlantic end. The second line of twenty vessels was a few miles nearer Gibraltar as a back-up to the first line.

The crew of the ship wondered what this was all about until we heard that some twenty-four hours before, four U-boats had been spotted travelling down together, off Portugal towards the Straits of Gibraltar, evidently hell-bent on entering the Mediterranean where our forces were turning the tide of the war. Our orders were to stop them getting into the Mediterranean by hook or by crook.

Following our arduous fourteen-day convoy trip, the crew were not properly rested before we were sent on this mission. We were mainly closed up at action stations as we patrolled in our line of ships, off Cape Trafalgar, with asdics and radar going. If these four U-boats got into the Mediterranean they could play havoc with Naval and merchant shipping.

After a fourteen-day convoy and little rest we were now at action stations for some twelve to fourteen hours and it was night-time. Suddenly, on the outside of the line, near Spain and Cape Trafalgar (the scene of Lord Nelson's famous victory over the French and Spanish Fleet in 1805) we saw gun flashes and heard the sound of depth charges. It was just before midnight. We later heard that two of the four U-boats had been sunk – two down and two to go.

Our next alert, shortly afterwards, was near the Moroccan Coast, and the port of Tangiers, following depth charges going off, and guns firing. When this died down, we learned that the other two U-boats, following depth charges, had surfaced under fire just outside Moroccan territorial waters and had raced into Tangiers harbour, a neutral port where they were allowed to stay under International Law for seventy-two hours. After this they had to leave or be interred for the duration of the war. A ring of warships was placed round Tangiers harbour, just outside territorial waters. This was a welcoming committee if the Germans decided to come out. My ship took up station on the edge of this screen nearest Gibraltar, and we patrolled with action stations standing down and with duty asdics/gun crews etc. standing the middle watch from twelve midnight to 4 a.m. Having been on duty all the previous day, following a fourteen-day convoy, and now another four hours to go before we got any sleep, we were whacked.

As petty officer I was second officer of the watch on the bridge, with a young sub lieutenant RNVR. We patrolled our sea area with asdics and radar going. It was difficult to keep awake at times, but by telling yarns and swigging hot, strong tea, we kept going.

At 4 a.m. we were due to be relieved by a Canadian lieutenant RNVR who was third senior officer on the ship with pre-war RNVR training. We watched the clock get to 4.15 a.m. and there was no sign of our relief officer of the watch. The sub lieutenant RNVR, like me, was getting wobbly with fatigue.

I said to him, 'I will go below and find out if Lieutenant S— has overslept.'

I left the bridge and made my way to the officer's cabin. On passing the wardroom door (officers' mess) I saw Lieutenant S— asleep on the wardroom table with an empty Gordon's gin bottle in his hand. (A new one.) I yelled in his ear to wake him up. He didn't move. I took the empty gin bottle from his hand put it on one side and (contrary to all Naval customs) I got hold of him and shook him very vigorously. (An unwritten law of the Royal Navy then was that you never physically got hold of a sleeping man. You tried everything in the book to rouse them, without touching them; only as a last resort did you grab them and shake them.)

When I shook Lieutenant S— and grabbed him he came to and in a slurred voice said, 'Wassamarrer' or that is what it sounded like. I knew he was a hard drinker like the captain, but did not expect this.

I said to him, 'It is nearly 4.30 a.m. and you were due to take over as officer of the watch on the bridge at 4 a.m. Sub Lieutenant — and I, now on watch, are very tired – can you take over as officer of the watch?'

Bleary eyed, he said, 'Corsh I can.' He added, 'I will be up in a minute.'

I went to the bridge, saw Sub Lieutenant — and he said to me, 'Did you find him?'

I said, 'Yes, sir, he was lying on the wardroom table having drunk a full bottle of Gordon's gin and he is on his way up here as pissed as a fiddler's bitch, to take over the watch.'

He said, 'He cannot take over the watch in that state.'

I said to him, 'Look, sir, you have not got much option. You and I are just about knackered, we cannot carry on without endangering the ship; you could call the captain and drop Lieutenant S— in the manure for being drunk on duty.' I added, 'The captain will be the same as Lieutenant S—. He cannot take over, the other officers have been through the mill duty-wise. We have no option. It is daylight, we are in the Straits of Gibraltar with other ships, relief radar, asdic, and gun crews closed up. He has only to pay attention to the second officer of the watch until he sobers up. It is getting on for five o'clock and we have been on our feet some nineteen to twenty hours non-stop.'

He reluctantly agreed. The Canadian lieutenant arrived on the bridge. He didn't appear to be too bad. We told him the situation and left the bridge to the call, 'I will be okay,' from him.

I went down to the NCOs' mess, got inside the door, and didn't bother to find my bunk, fully clothed I flopped on the first wooden bench I came to and fell asleep in seconds. I had not been asleep for more than fifteen to twenty minutes before I was awakened by an almighty crash, and the sound of tearing metal. The ship laid over at an angle of some forty-five degrees and I nearly fell off my sleeping bench.

My first thoughts on trying to awake were that the subs must have got out of Tangiers and one of them had torpedoed us. I struggled up the ladder to the upper deck, still not properly awake, and on reaching the upper deck I blew up my inflatable lifebelt, which was round my chest. (The Navy drill was – one blow for the wife, one blow for the children, and one blow for yourself.) I got one foot on the side of the ship ready to jump over into the sea but then realised the ship was still floating. I looked along the upper deck in the dawn light and I realised that all the upper deck was still there. If a torpedo had hit a small ship like this, half of it would be missing. I got down the ship's side and ran to the front (bow) of the ship and stopped on the upper deck. The ship's engines had ceased to function. I looked towards the Moroccan coast and it was dark. I looked towards the Spanish coast on the other side of the Straits of Gibraltar and it was broad daylight and sunshine. I looked up in the air at an angle of forty-five to fifty degrees and saw brilliant sunshine over the top of a mountain, I then realised we were almost on the beach in Morocco and realised that with the rocks not far away, we must have hit one. The ship was still floating and had regained deeper water.

I went below to the crews' quarters and everybody was still asleep, although not for long. I yelled, shook and roused them from their bunks, and shouted to them to screw down the watertight hatches in the crews' compartment, where, although closed at sea, the water was gushing round the closed doors showing that the lower compartments were already flooded. This was soon done and with the ship's pumps going we were still afloat. I next went to the officers' cabins to make sure they were all awake and aware of the situation. On arrival in the first lieutenant's cabin, a lieutenant RNVR, the ship's second in command, I found he was still asleep. In view of the situation I grabbed him and shook him.

He woke up irritably and snarled at me, 'What is wrong, what do you want?'

I said to him, 'Look over the side of your bunk, sir.'

He did so and saw that water was round my waist and nearly up to him. He said, 'What has happened?'

I said, 'The ship is sinking, sir, you had better get up on deck.'

He needed no second telling, he was up and gone. Having made sure nobody was asleep down below, I made my way to the upper deck. A mayday signal had been made and nearby boats came to our help.

The first boat alongside to help was a large modern sloop, the flotilla leader of another escort group commanded by a full Royal Naval captain who leaned on the side of his bridge overlooking our small corvette, surveying all our bridge and upper deck. Just before she came alongside, the first lieutenant had ordered me to get the 'collision mat' out, a large twelve feet by twelve feet canvas mat which was pulled over where you thought the hole was, to provide a temporary ship's hull patch. I knew some three large compartments in the bottom of the ship were holed so this thing was a waste of time. I told the first lieutenant this but he insisted it had to be done. Our captain, on the bridge by this time, had ordered the officers' stewards to bring up all the booze from the wardroom: spirits, wines, beer, etc. He had pulled all the signal flags out of their lockers and replaced each flag with a bottle of booze and was inciting all officers and men to drink the lot before the ship went down, saying, 'We don't want all this booze to go to the bottom, what a waste, help yourselves.'

When the sloop came alongside she put her powerful suction pumps hoses into our flooded compartments and pumped like hell. Then we were just holding our own, the water was not rising inside the ship. In the confusion with stopped engines, the ship's stokers decided to break into the ship's rum store and were soon pie-eyed. This lot were mainly fugitives from the Royal Navy Glasshouse at Maidstone, Kent (Detention Centre Royal Navy). I saw what was developing and I got all the seamen under me, and the NCOs and told them that if I even suspected they had been near booze I would have their testicles for a necktie. As far as I was aware, they all behaved and I watched them most of the time; none of the seamen had any drink.

I took three or four senior hands with me, able seamen, and went down below to survey how the ship was standing up to the water pressure of flooded compartments. In the ship's main boiler room was one of the ship's main bulkheads (wall of steel) designed to make the ship watertight in order to stay afloat if the main hull was damaged and water got in. The water in the boiler room was some four to five feet deep, but to my horror I saw the steel wall was bulging badly in several places, indicating that the compartment on the other side was completely flooded. If the bulkhead (wall) collapsed the ship would go down in minutes. I shouted to my assistants to get timber four inch by four inch, six inch by six inch, and I measured the distance between the bulging bulkhead and the back of the ship's main boiler, the only support; it was about three feet.

I got my lads to cut the timber into three-feet lengths, and cut squares off two-inch thick planks in order to reinforce the ends of the square timber, and to put at each end of the support timbers to stop the bulkhead being pierced by the support timber. These supports now had to be put in place, the water was almost up to my neck, I got into the space, about three feet between the collapsing wall and the still red-hot boiler. I systematically inserted some twelve to fifteen supports between the bulkhead (wall) and the boiler. As I put the supports in, the steel wall was bulging round the supports, I knew that if the wall collapsed I would not get out of that three feet wide space. Up to my neck in water I would be pinned between the wall and the boiler. I did not let my assistants come in with me as it was too dangerous – they threw me the wood or handed me the tools, saws, wedges, hammers, etc. When I had finished in the boiler room, burned a bit by the hot boiler, and waterlogged, I made my way to other vital points in the ship and shored up more walls with timber to reinforce them against the weight of water on the other side.

On return to the upper deck and daylight, I saw a large old Navy dockyard paddle tug, a really powerful vessel from Gibraltar dockyard, coming alongside. She was soon secured to the opposite side to the sloop, and my ship was slung, supported between the two. The paddle tug put her powerful suction pumps down inside our ship's hull, and then slung two ARP-type fire pumps on board. These were soon started up and the water inside our ship started to go down.

The sloop and the paddle tug working together then propelled our ship towards Gibraltar, some forty miles away, with an anti-submarine escort. All seemed to be getting under control when I heard a disturbance on the upper deck, just behind our funnel. I went to see what was going on. To my dismay and horror I saw the ship's old cook stripped to the waist like an old-time prize fighter (bare knuckle type), as drunk as a fiddler's bitch, squaring up to the captain who was likewise attired, except he had his shirt on. He was squaring up to the cook, going round and round; each time they tried to hit each other they were so drunk they nearly fell over. They were addressing each other in rather unfriendly terms in loud voices. Cook to Captain: 'I don't want some shortarsed cargo-busting, Merchant Navy type bastard telling me what to do.' Captain to Cook: 'I have dealt with bloody hash slingers like you before, I will knock your f— block off.'

I was nonplussed, none of our other ship's officers were present and it was clear among the sober members of the crew who watched, that they expected me to do something. I looked up at the bridge of the sloop alongside, saw the captain RN looking down at me, and thought, What must he think of this lot? This was not my Royal Navy, disciplined, reliable, ready for any situation. I was just going to restrain the boxers when a young lieutenant stepped on board from the sloop.

He said, 'I am the first lieutenant of the ship next door, my captain has sent me on board to assume command. You are the chief bosun's mate of this ship?'

I replied rather thankfully, 'Yes, sir.'

He then said, 'Arrest your commanding officer and remove him to his quarters and lock him in. Place a sentry on the locked door with the keys, with orders to stay there to let him out in case this ship goes down. Impress on the sentry that he must not leave his post under any circumstances.'

I saluted, replied, 'Yes, sir,' called a couple of able seamen as escort and went up to our drunken commanding officer who was still trying to fight the cook. I and the able seamen restrained him, told him he was being arrested and what for, and on whose orders; the air was blue, he was going to fight everybody. We propelled him to his cabin (fitted with toilets, bunks, tables, chairs, etc.), pushed him inside and locked the door, to the strains of, 'I will have you lot court martialled for assault on an officer.'

I posted a sentry as instructed and returned to the new temporary commanding officer, who said, 'Now show me round the ship, and all that has been done to save her.'

I gave him a conducted tour of the ship, showed him what I had done, and all other steps. He appeared very satisfied, congratulated me and went off to find the other officers. (The cook had also been locked up by this time.) It was not very long before the ships arrived in Gibraltar. The sloop and tug got us as near as they dared to our dockside berth before one of them cast off to allow us to get alongside the dockyard wall, where more pumps were lined up, ready to stem the rising water inside our badly holed craft.

The next order I got was to get all depth charges, ammunition, etc. off the ship as soon as possible as there was an empty dry dock available to take the ship nearby and, as there were only three in Gibraltar, it might be urgently required for a bigger, more important ship at very short notice.

We got all the available ammunition etc. off the ship in double-quick time. We could not empty the main magazine as it was flooded. (Not much danger from ammunition underwater.) When ready, the dock was flooded, the gates opened, we were berthed just outside the dock gates and pulled in by wire hawsers, after pumps on the dockside had been removed from the ship. They had just got her in position in the middle of the dock, where they wanted her, had closed the lock gates, and had partly pumped out the dock, when she sunk on to the bottom of the dock. We all heaved a sigh of relief.

The lieutenant RNVR who had skilfully hit the submerged rock at eighteen knots in his inebriated state, mistaking it for a submarine despite being told by the duty asdic operator that it was not a submarine, insisted – even after the incident – he had attacked a U-boat. (Luckily he had not fired depth charges as the ship hit the submerged rock.)

After the dry dock was pumped out, I went to the bottom of the dock to look at the damage to the hull. There was a gash in the bottom of the ship which started about one third of the way from the ship's bow to the stern (her length) and continued for twenty-two feet parallel with her keel some three feet away from it, damaging three or four watertight compartments, nothing like submarine ramming damage. In addition to this, in the end of this large gash in the ship's bottom was wedged a lump of rock about twenty pounds in weight. With a crowbar I got it out of the hole, and carried it to the wardroom, where I presented the Canadian lieutenant RNVR with it, saying, 'Here, sir, is a piece of your rammed submarine, which I have just removed from the ship's bottom.' (The air was blue.)

Several days later, when things had quietened down, it was approaching Christmas, 1941. I was working on the upper deck of my ship. (The inebriated commanding officer had taken over command again and a court martial was pending.) I almost fell over when I saw, coming on board, the engineer vice-admiral in charge of Gibraltar Dockyard. Such an important chap as this arriving, I wondered what was happening. As we were in dock, we were excused the usual bullshit of formal senior officer visits. I went up to him – he was in full uniform (not mufti).

I saluted, stood to attention, and said, 'Good morning, sir, I will fetch the captain.'

He saluted back and said, 'No, don't do that. I am having a quiet walk round my domain. You can show me round.' After a pause, he said, 'I have heard of the ship's mishap the other day, and I was advised to go and have a quiet look. I am interested in the steps taken to prevent this ship being lost.' (I was rather puzzled at what this member of the heavy mob was up to.) He said, 'Show me round.'

I took him all over the ship, and showed him my amateur attempts at shoring up the ship's walls with timber. In the boiler room he asked me who got between the bulkhead (wall) and the boiler to put the supports in. (They were all still in place, nothing had been touched since we arrived in dock.) He went all over the ship and even viewed the damage to the ship's bottom.

He eventually went to leave the ship. I stood at the gangway with him, he shook hands with me and said, 'There is no doubt in my mind that your skilful action with shoring timber and limited resources saved this ship from going down. If this had been the result of enemy action they would have awarded you a medal as big as a coal-hole lid, but as it was caused by one of your own officers you will get nothing. Well done my lad, keep up the good work.' He then left the ship.

We all knew on the ship that a court martial was pending and I was rather surprised, about three to four days before the hearing, when I was approached by a young able seaman in the crew who asked me if he could seek advice. I took him on one side and said, 'What is the problem?'

He then said, 'As you know, I was the helmsman on the ship's wheel when we hit the rock.'

I said, 'Yes I know that, what is wrong?'

He replied, 'Lieutenant S— who was officer of the watch when we hit the rock, has approached me and offered me £100 cash to testify at the court martial that I was steering a course one hundred and eighty degrees from the real one I was on, and I really do not know what to do.' This young man's daily pay in those days, 1941, was 3/6d old money. (Today's rate about 18p.) He had never been in danger of receiving £100 from any source, and was not likely to be.

I said to him, 'Your choice is quite simple. You have never been in any trouble that I know of and therefore you have a good name, which is valuable. Lieutenant S— is a very rich man in Canada where he lives and, whatever happens, he is not bothered about you. You must think of your good name and when you give your evidence tell the truth, and nothing else. The president of the court martial is Admiral of the Fleet, Sir Andrew Cunningham C in C Mediterranean Fleet; he has forgotten more about navigation than you and I will ever know. If you go before him at the court martial and give false evidence, you will finish up in the glasshouse [military prison]. You please yourself, but think about what good your £100 will do you when your character is in ruins and you are doing three to six months in the glasshouse for perjury – it is not worth it.'

He said, 'Thank you,' and went off. (For some reason I was not called to give evidence at the court martial in Gibraltar.) The captain was found guilty and was dismissed from his ship with disgrace. Lieutenant S— was also found guilty and dismissed from his ship with disgrace.

I never found out why I never heard of the captain again, but Lieutenant S— was appointed to a larger ship (a cruiser) with a better position than he had on our ill-fated corvette, which he demolished.

Our poor old corvette was so badly damaged that it would take some three to four months to repair, so she was dragged off to a place of rest whilst repairs were carried out. Our crew, including me, were put in the reserve pool of crew members in the local base at Gibraltar to act as spare parts for the Mediterranean Fleet. After about a week to a fortnight, I was appointed to a Mediterranean Fleet destroyer, a real Royal Navy command, and was I glad to be back with the real Navy where I knew what to expect (most of the time).

Submarine Warfare

The year was 1941, the U-boat war was at its height. It was evident that we were not winning, in fact we were not far short of losing. A British destroyer had with others escorted a large convoy from the Straits of Gibraltar and turned south down the coast of Africa. Everything seemed to be all right, and after a few days steaming south with the convoy down the coast of Africa, the old destroyer turned round and headed back northwards towards Gibraltar and its base, where she was needed more than where she was.

As she virtually backtracked on her previous course, all alone, it was assumed she would have an uneventful return to base. About twenty-four hours into her new course it was a sunny afternoon with a stiff breeze and a choppy sea with white horses on the wave tops.

On the bridge of the destroyer was the officer of the watch, a lieutenant RNVR, with look-outs and other personnel. The ship's asdics (anti-submarine detector gear) were pinging away on the amplifying gear for all to hear.

Suddenly, a port-side look-out, a young ordinary seaman, yelled, 'Submarine periscope bearing red [port] forty-five degrees travelling left to right range [distance] about six miles.'

The lieutenant RNVR walked over to him and said, 'You would never see a submarine periscope in this choppy water six miles away.'

The look-out, an officer candidate under training, said rather disdainfully in his five-pound-note accent, 'I saw a submarine periscope.'

The officer ran to a voice-pipe and called the captain of the destroyer, a commander RN to the bridge. He told him of the report, and the captain immediately altered the course of the ship to cross the direction of the reported submarine's line of travel. After covering some three to four miles the amplified asdic equipment on the bridge changed from an outgoing ping on its own, to this plus an incoming ping, the sure sign of something there, an underwater object.

Action stations were sounded, all guns, depth charges, and torpedo tubes were manned and brought to the ready state the petty officer HSD (Higher Submarine Detector operator) was in his 'cabinet' in the bowels of the ship, in contact with the ship's captain on the bridge by phone. He reported that it was a definite submarine contact and not a shoal of fish or sunken vessel on the seabed, and gave a distance and bearing of the object. The captain on the bridge compass platform conned the ship on to the direction of the target, and ordered all engines full speed ahead.

'Stand by to fire depth charges.'

The ship roared over the target and when the noise of the outgoing ping was almost the same as the asdic incoming ping on the asdic gear, the captain shouted down his phone to the depth charge crew on the stern, 'Fire.' At this order they dropped six 300 lb. depth charges off the stern (set to certain depths). Two charges were also fired from the port and starboard depth charge throwers, making ten 300 lb. charges in all (3,000 lbs. of TNT).

After a good few seconds, this little lot exploded in the depths of the ocean. The captain turned the ship after the attack, and pointed the bow (front) towards the boiling sea where the charges had gone off. After a few minutes nothing came up. The petty officer HSD confirmed from his cabinet to the captain that the sub was still there where it had been attacked. The captain gave repeat orders to attack again. This was done and again the target did not come up. After some five to six attacks, the captain, an Atlantic veteran and destroyer commander, decided it could not be a submarine. Only five depth charges were left on board and he gave the order to resume patrol to Gibraltar.

He stood on the bridge, rather disappointed that he had not got a submarine 'kill' (confirmed by bodies, debris, the sunken boat etc.), when there was a commotion at the top of the bridge ladder. Everybody on the bridge was wondering what the hell was going on, when the petty officer HSD ran on to the bridge, confronted the captain and, in a loud clear voice, pointing an index finger at him, said, 'I don't care what happens to me, sir, but if you leave that submarine down there with depth charges still on this ship I will personally report you to the admiral when we return to Gibraltar. You know the orders we had prior to this trip.' (Nobody else knew what these were.)

Everybody who could hear what was going on held their breath. For an NCO to confront and threaten his commanding officer in action, in time of war, was beyond comprehension. The captain looked at the petty officer HSD and said, 'Do you think you can do any better than I have done?'

Everybody within earshot held their breath.

The petty officer said, 'I couldn't do much worse.'

The captain stepped down from the compass platform and said to the irate petty officer HSD, 'The ship is yours now, see what you can do.'

The petty officer climbed on to the compass platform and called to his assistant asdic operator down below, 'Give me a range and a bearing [direction] of the sub.'

He got his information, gave orders to the ship's quartermaster on the steering wheel, to get the ship on course to pass over the target, and ordered the engine room for full speed on the engines. He gave orders to the depth charge crews by phone to set the remaining five depth charges to the deepest depth setting possible, and 'stand by to fire them'. The destroyer roared in over the target, the HSD petty officer was listening to the asdic gear, as was his assistant, and at the appropriate time, the petty officer shouted to the depth charge crews (by phone), 'Fire.' The last five charges went over the side and it seemed an eternity before, in the depths of the ocean, there was a muffled boom, boom, as they all went off.

The captain in the meantime was leaning on the side of the bridge; he had a laconic smile on his face whilst waiting for the depth charges to go off. He looked at the petty officer on the compass platform after his submarine attack, as much as to say, 'Who is the clever bugger now?'

After some minutes, the boiling sea where the last set of charges went down suddenly became calmer, and a large ocean-going Italian submarine broke surface. Cheers rang out from the destroyer's crew, and orders were given for all guns to open fire on the target. All the guns 4.7-inch, 20 mm Oerlikons, and Pom-Poms raked the submarine, but as the submarine hatches opened, the crew poured out on deck yelling in Italian that they were surrendering, and the guns were ordered to cease fire.

The Italian crew were picked up; her captain had activated her scuttling charges and after some ten minutes the sub blew up and sunk.

(When she was sunk she had just got into the Atlantic from Italy, she had a full complement of twenty-two torpedoes ready to fire, and had passed through the Straits of Gibraltar to follow the convoy the destroyer had left, prior to the sinking, and to wreak as much havoc as possible on African convoys.)

The Italian captain of the submarine revealed after his capture that the first pattern of depth charges from the destroyer had jammed all his controls – he could not surface but was slowly sinking. Subsequent charges just sent him deeper, but he said, 'The last pattern fired exploded right underneath us, blew us to the surface and saved us from a watery grave.' (The pattern fired by the petty officer HSD.)

The British destroyer of First World War vintage (1916) with a full war complement of some one hundred and sixty men, was a bit overcrowded with the Italian sub-crew. The Italian sub-crew all had crabs, scabies, skin diseases, VD etc. They were so short of trained submariners that despite what was wrong with them they had to go to sea in their submarines when required. (Needless to say our lads contracted most of these diseases whilst returning to Gibraltar with the Italian crew, except of course for VD.)

After this gallant action, the captain of the destroyer was awarded the DSO, the lookout who spotted the submarine was awarded the DSM. The hero of the plot, the petty officer HSD was awarded a medal and promoted to warrant officer in the field, a battle honour which could not be taken away, except if one committed some diabolical crime. (He was lucky when you think what he got up to, threatening his commanding officer etc. in action in wartime.)

Taranto (1943)

In 1943, after various Allied successes in North Africa (including the defeat of General Rommel) the capture of Sicily, and the relief of Malta, Italy decided the cards were stacked against her and decided to surrender. I was with a large Naval task force (Force 'H') including aircraft carriers, battleships, cruisers, destroyers, minesweepers, tank landing craft, heading for Taranto and the surrender of the main Italian battle fleet. They had many fine, fast modern ships which it would be nice to get into Allied hands in order to avoid other complications of them falling into German hands.

The Allied task force headed in towards Taranto harbour, our minesweepers clearing a channel ahead; as mines popped up we destroyed them with gunfire and steadily moved towards the harbour. The situation on shore was somewhat confused. Nobody knew who was in charge of the shore batteries covering the harbour, Germans or Italians. Was the large heavily armed Italian Navy going to come out and surrender or was this a ruse to lure our heavy ships within gun range and come out with all guns blazing? We moved towards Taranto harbour with some trepidation, but knowing the Italian Navy, whom we had tried to get to come out and fight throughout the war without success, we doubted a ruse on their part. Where were the Germans? Who was in charge? Were we moving into a huge trap?

Admiral Cunningham (John), in command of the force, played a softly, softly approach, ready for virtually anything. My ship was an old First World War-built boat from 1916, HMS *Wishart*. We were in the vanguard of the force approaching Taranto Harbour, and we did not know what to expect if we went in – gunfire or cheers. We were soon to find out. As an old destroyer we were ordered to enter Taranto Harbour to see what would happen.

Many Italians were on the dockside waving and cheering as we went slowly in. Was this a welcome, or were German soldiers behind them with fixed bayonets and guns, threatening mayhem if they gave the game away? Before they could wreak havoc on our ships.

We went in at very slow speed past the Italian crowds only 50–60 yards away but with everything 'ready to go', guns fully loaded, engine room tuned for high speed. We crept into the harbour and nothing happened. We made a circuit of the harbour, everything ready. Not a shot was fired and after some time our captain reported to the Admiral by signal that it appeared all clear.

The British fleet prepared to enter Taranto Harbour with troops, guns, vehicles and men. At the same time we saw the most impressive sight, one I shall always remember. Leaving Taranto Harbour anchorage was the Italian battle fleet, flags of surrender flying at their mastheads to be met by British ships to accept the surrender and escort them to Malta. What a sight.

Just before the war, all round the Mediterranean, where British warships were in port with Italian warships on courtesy visits, the Italians were always crowing and agitating British sailors in local bars and cafés as to how they were waiting for war to start under Mussolini (Il Duce) and how their Navy would sweep the British

Navy out of the *Mare Nostrum*. Many a good punch up ensued, but it was a different story when war started; they always disappeared over the horizon at the first signs of a fight. (They were so fast our ships could not get to grips with them.)

My destroyer made another attempt to make sure the harbour was safe for our big ships to enter by being ordered to go in and round the harbour again by the Admiral. The Italian civilians were still on the harbour walls cheering, but we were in the direct firing line if the Germans held the shore batteries and had been 'playing possum' the first time round. As we entered the second time, we were ordered to shed our boiler suits to reveal our white uniforms underneath, and fall in by our guns to impress the Italians on the quays. (We all thought, What a load of bullshit. If the Germans held the shore batteries we would be killed if we revealed boiler suits or whites.)

We made a second circuit of the harbour, watching the hills and cliffs around it for puffs of smoke indicating we were under fire from shore batteries, but all was quiet. The larger ships followed us in, guns at the ready, but all was quiet. We thought that if the big ships were not fired on we must be okay.

After entering harbour in the afternoon, we were ordered to anchor just inside the Italian boom vessel which opened and closed the boom to let craft in and out of the harbour. The boom was a system of floating spikes and nets to deter, catch or damage MTBs, submarines or underwater swimmers, and was controlled by the crew of the boom defence vessel. The vessel opened and closed the boom gate like a huge trapdoor in metal mesh nets covering the entrance to the harbour to let in or keep out all intruders.

We were instructed whilst on guard duty by the Admiral in command that nothing was to come into the harbour and nothing to go out unless he authorised it, and to watch the Italian boom defence vessel and what they got up to opening and closing the harbour. We appreciated his concern with the heavy tonnage of Royal Navy ships, supply ships, tank landing craft etc. in the harbour. A pair of enemy Italian–German torpedo boats or gunboats in the harbour at this time could wreak havoc.

Evening came, darkness closed in, and it appeared, late in the evening, that things were reasonably quiet, no German air attacks, no trouble, and we relaxed a little. About 10 p.m. I was on watch with my gun crew, a 4.7-inch gun trained on the boom defence vessel and ready to go. I was the NCO in command of the gun. Suddenly, out to sea, I heard the roar of very powerful motor boats with MTB-type engines. They were coming in at high speed towards the harbour entrance. The boom defence vessel (Italian) came to life, and the boom started to open to let these unknown craft in. In the dark we were rather unsure whether the boom was opening or not, then I saw it was.

I shouted to a fellow NCO nearby, 'Man the Oerlikons!' We had a 20 mm Oerlikon gun, one each side of the bridge, not far from where we were. We got to the guns at the same time, and I shouted to him, 'A short burst over the boom defence vessel.' We drew a bead over the wheelhouse of the boom defence vessel's control room, and we both fired at the same time. The tracer bullets skimmed the wheelhouse of the boom defence craft and lo and behold, the boom started to close again at high speed. We swung our 20 mm Oerlikon guns around towards the channel entering the harbour and, shouting at each other, we controlled the tracer shells from our guns in order to criss-cross the channel into the harbour. The loud roaring MTB-type engines got louder, but suddenly the noise receded, indicating that the boats at the last minute had turned away at high speed, and were heading out to sea from Taranto harbour, with engines at full blast.

I returned to my gun crew and had a cup of tea and sat down. I suddenly remembered at about 11 p.m. that I had rescued from the galley (Cookhouse) earlier in the day a container full of fresh beef stew, carrots and peas with the intention of heating it up on the cookhouse stove during the night for my gun crew.

I went to collect the pot with the stew from the floor of the chief and petty officers' mess, where it should have been with the lid on. When I picked it up, the lid was off, lying on the floor. I put the lid on, went up to the cookhouse with the utensil and heated it on the stove. No light could be shown, it was in a war zone and a candle light was only just possible. Having heated the stew, with a fistful of mugs, I took it up to my gun crew and distributed it. At 11.30 p.m. on a cold night it was most acceptable. A couple of the gun crew drinking soup said to me, 'That was lovely but what are those tasty crinkly bits you get in your soup?'

I suggested celery seeds. They ate it all, I saved some for myself and on taking my ration to the cookhouse to warm it up, I heated it on the stove and, as it was bubbling, I saw in the bottom of the pot a brown mass of boiled cockroaches. I now knew why they were talking about the 'tasty crinkly bits' in the soup. I threw it all away, kept quiet and that was that. (All HM ships were infested with cockroaches at all times; if one left a tin of milk, jam or treacle open before you knew where you were it was jammed with dying cockroaches. (Somebody had knocked the lid off my late night stew and it was soon full of cockroaches hell-bent on suicide.)

It was about midnight or just after, in Taranto Harbour that night in 1943, and we were chatting round the duty gun, when there was a terrific explosion, the sky lit up and the echoes reverberated round the harbour. We all jumped up, the boom was closed, nothing moved, and an eerie silence descended on the harbour. We sensed, knew, something drastic had happened.

We had not long to wait before we found out. A message was received to the effect that HMS *Abdiel*, a large mine-laying destroyer anchored in the harbour, had blown up. Due to the excessive amount of Royal Navy ships in the harbour, somebody decided on who should berth at the quayside in Taranto to unload soldiers, vehicles, ammunition etc., trying to get priorities right to continue the successful push by the Allies from the bottom end of Italy, northwards. It was decided that HMS *Abdiel*, with her valuable cargo of some four hundred red devils, the paratroopers with their ammunition and vehicles on her empty mine decks, should anchor in the harbour to wait, as all wharves were full and she was about the only ship that could not berth on arrival in Taranto Harbour.

After the huge explosion which had blinded and deafened ships' crews over a great distance, the order went out to all ships nearby to send motor launches, lifeboats, and all rescue boats to the area where *Abdiel* had been anchored; the sea was alive with rescue craft but to no avail. I took charge of a lifeboat from my destroyer and criss-crossed the area several times, but apart from a dead Royal Navy stoker whose body was recovered, there was nothing, just matchwood and fine debris, all that was left of this fine ship and her temporary cargo of paras. There were very few, if any, survivors of Naval or military personnel. The scene was very confused and as we could not do any good I took my lifeboat back to the ship, and we were hoisted.

Speculation was rife in the fleet as to how and what sunk the *Abdiel*, an efficient fast modern mine-layer. The favourite answer was that she was anchored over a minefield, controlled by push button from ashore in Taranto and the Italians/Germans pushed the button as she swung round her anchor in the harbour. We never did find out what did sink her.

When the shouting, noise and tumult ceased, my captain received a message from the Admiral in command that we were to 'anchor over the remains of the *Abdiel* for the night and post upper deck sentries, and look-outs, with small depth charges to prevent Italian/German underwater swimmers from getting at her secret papers in her safes and strongrooms'. One can imagine the rather peculiar feeling in everybody's guts when we were ordered to anchor over the wreck of the *Abdiel* for the night. Was there another controlled mine or mines nearby? We all knew controlled mines were anchored more or less in a line and could be detonated from a control point.

Strangely enough, nobody slept very soundly that night. A lot of Naval war veterans, like myself, slept on the upper deck with our life jackets inflated, as, if we went up in any explosion, if we woke up, we would be ready to swim for it.

The night passed more or less uneventfully. The following day we were relieved of our watch over *Abdiel*, as Royal Navy divers and other bodies took over dealing with the sunken warship and secret material. My ship was then ordered by the admiral to resume 'riding shotgun' on the Italian boom defence vessel controlling entry to Taranto Harbour.

It was about 10 a.m. after our hectic night, and I was the duty NCO on the upper deck of my destroyer in the harbour. There was a sound of very powerful ship's engines approaching the harbour, it was a bit misty. I had the duty guns manned in case of emergency, covering the channel into the harbour.

Out of the mist, one behind the other, came two, large, fast, modern Italian Corvettes. They had their surrender flags flying at the masthead. We gave them permission to come in. They both anchored not far from my ship and one of them lowered a large fast motor launch, with an officer in the stern, which came over to my destroyer. The launch came alongside, an Italian Naval Commander, dark haired, well-groomed and very well-dressed, came up the gangway. I accorded him the courtesy of his rank as per Royal Navy standards and saluted as he stepped on deck.

He walked over to me, shook hands and said, 'I have come to surrender my ship and crew to you, can I speak to your commanding officer?'

I said, 'Yes, I will go and fetch him.'

I had noticed that the Italian commander spoke 'perfect American'. As I turned to go and fetch our commanding officer, I said to him, 'Excuse me, you sound like an American with your speech.'

He smiled and said, 'I am an American.'

I looked dubiously at him and his uniform, pointed to his ship and said, 'How come you were fighting against them?'

He smiled and said, 'It is a bit complicated but briefly, I was born in America of Italian parents. I was brought up and went to school in America. My parents have land, property, cash in Italy and so has my family. Before America entered the war, Mussolini spread the word in the

States that all men of military age who were Italian (my father was Italian) must return to Italy and join the Italian Forces. Anybody who did not do so would have all family money, land, property, possessions seized by the Italian Government, whether they lived in Italy or abroad.' He added, 'My family in America and Italy have large estates, money invested, and property. I had no option (under pressure from family) but come back and join the Italian Forces.'

I said something like, 'Bloody hell. What a dilemma to be in.'

He replied, 'Exactly, I am very glad this lot is all over.'

I led him down to the officers' wardroom and introduced him to my commanding officer. They shook hands, and I added to the commanding officer, 'His ship is nearby, he wants to surrender.'

My commanding officer said to him, 'You are a bit late coming into harbour?'

The Italian-American replied, 'Yes, I tried to come in last night but a boat guarding the harbour entrance opened up with gunfire on my ship, and my other flotilla member and we had to retire at high speed back to sea.'

I said to the captain, 'That was me, sir, our orders were no ships in or out.'

He replied, 'Yes I understand.' Then he had a drink with the Italian commanding officer, who, when he left our ship an hour or more later, was merry.

In the aftermath to the *Abdiel*, a Royal Navy diver was sent down to check the wreck the next day. When he came up, he was not very eager to go back down again, I understand. Evidently he looked into the mine decks of the *Abdiel* where the paras and their vehicles were, and apparently they were still all lined up on the mine deck as if ready to disembark; they were all standing up along the mine deck, apparently weighed down at the bottom by Army boots and gaiters, all swaying in motion by the action of the water. As if they were still alive.)

The Captain's Bicycle

In the year 1938, I was a serving (seventeen-year old) seaman on one of His Majesty's ships, in the American West Indies Squadron, based in Bermuda, the main port being on Ireland Island, the Royal Naval Dockyard. At this time there were no trains, buses, cars, lorries, motorcycles, coaches, planes etc. All mechanically propelled vehicles were taboo, forbidden on the island and were non-existent.

The only forms of travel were shank's pony (your flat feet), bicycles, horse and carriage, boat, and life was fairly tranquil as far as noise, pollution, etc. were concerned. We had only just arrived on this Royal Naval station and were not quite sure what to do, or where to go, or how to get there.

The capital, Hamilton was some eighteen or nineteen miles from the dockyard by road, about five or six miles across the water by liberty boat, from the ship. The boats from the ship were most infrequent in order to discourage visits by Royal Navy personnel to the capital, Hamilton, which was grossly anti-Royal Navy, but welcomed all sorts of American cruise-liner characters who caused more trouble than anybody at times.

The main means of transport was the bicycle. These were in short supply in Bermuda, and of course how could we, on 2/– per day (10p new money), hope to buy a £10 or £5 bicycle?

The padre on our ship had managed to acquire a rather dilapidated green Raleigh bicycle for his own use as transport on the island, and was generous enough to loan it to members of the crew who wanted to travel on the islands, to Hamilton or elsewhere, if he was not using it.

On the day in question, two able seamen, Cockney characters, wished to visit Hamilton, the capital. One said to the other, 'I wonder if the parson is using his old bike today, the lads reckon he will lend it to you if he is not going to use it.'

They both agreed to seek out the parson and request the use of his old bike. They found him in his cabin, respectfully asked to borrow his cycle for the rest of the day and the dear old parson said, 'I am not using it, help yourselves, you will find it in the officers' cycle rack at the bottom of the officers' gangway. It is a gents' green Raleigh cycle, with three-speed etc. When you have finished put it back in the cycle rack.'

They departed, found the cycle rack near the officers' gangway on the quayside, saw a green Raleigh pedal cycle three-speed etc., removed it from the cycle rack, and one sat on the crossbar of the cycle while the other pedalled and steered.

They were bound for Hamilton. They travelled along the dockside, wobbling from side to side, and as they reached the dockyard gates, about half a mile away, there was a flurry at the officers' gangway. Orders were shouted by Royal Marines, bugles were sounded, bosun's pipes shrilled, and the captain of the ship emerged, down the gangway, and all hell was let loose. The captain appeared displeased as he strode to the officers' cycle rack at the bottom of the gangway to get his only form of transport, a new green Raleigh pedal cycle, delivered some two days before, to ride it to his newly rented home nearby. It was gone. The irate commanding officer let out a roar as he glanced towards the dockyard gates about half a mile away and saw his new cycle being ridden towards Hamilton by two of his able seamen. He could do nothing, and shouting by all and sundry did not help, as they were too far away. A furious captain decided to walk home, with dire threats as to what he would do to the two reprobates when they returned.

That evening the two able seamen were returning from shore leave on the captain's brand-new cycle; they were full of beer, etc., and one sat on the crossbar, one pedalled (in the time-honoured fashion). Suddenly they reached the top of a rather steep hill on the road from Hamilton to the dockyard, at the bottom of which was a ninety degree bend flanked by a six-foot wall.

Apparently they descended this hill at a terrific speed, did not make the bend, and hit the wall at the bottom, with disastrous results to the captain's cycle. The front wheel looked like a figure-of-eight knot, and both men were slightly injured but, helped by local residents, they went on their way, carrying the remains of the captain's cycle on their shoulders.

As they entered the dockyard they were arrested, brought to the ship, cycle as well, or what was left of it. They sent for the padre who was most sympathetic on hearing they had mistaken his old green Raleigh bike for the captain's new one. He had given permission for them to use his bike and after his representations to the captain, he (the captain) saw sense and agreed not 'to hang' the culprits for theft etc., but merely let them pay for the extensive repairs to his new cycle from their pay, which took several months.

The Captain's Chef

In about 1948–49 the large modern destroyer I was serving in as a chief petty officer was somewhere in Scotland, near Lossiemouth. We were doing crash boat duties with a large fleet aircraft carrier which was training Royal Naval Voluntary Reserve pilots on their annual training stint for a fortnight. Daily we followed the carrier to sea and when any aircraft did not make it, either taking off or landing, and finished in the sea, our job was to rescue the crew.

We had been at this for several days when flying conditions deteriorated and the carrier stayed in harbour, as did we. Our captain, a senior naval commander of long experience, had an invite to go ashore on a local Scottish estate, to do some trout and salmon fishing which he was fond of.

He departed in the ship's launch at about 5 p.m., complete with his fly-fishing gear. About 1 a.m. he returned, tired, damp, but rather happy as he had caught two salmon trout in the local waters. One fish was about 2 lb. the other 1½ lb. in weight. The captain put them in the officers' galley (cookhouse) and left a note to the chef instructing that one was to be prepared for his 10.30 a.m. breakfast. He then retired to his bunk, happily thinking of fresh steamed salmon trout for his breakfast. (It took some three to four hours of wet and cold to catch them, but all would be worth it at breakfast.)

Just prior to this incident, the captain's old chef had finished his time in the Navy, and a newly fledged officers' cook had taken his place, straight from Royal Navy Barracks, Chatham and the cookery school.

The captain slept soundly, then got up and dressed at about 10 a.m., in preparation for his fishy feast at 10.30 a.m. sharp. When ready and at about the right time, he rang the bell for his chef to produce a fish gourmet's delight. The young man marched into the skipper's cabin with a large silver salver, complete with lid, which he placed on the table in front of the captain, together with a cruet of salt, vinegar and pepper.

The captain was absorbed by the silver salver. He lifted the lid and there lay a beautiful salmon trout, encased in thick dark brown-black crispy batter, almost burnt, with only head and tail removed. The old man nearly had a stroke, he virtually yelled at the young chef, 'What the hell do you call this?'

The chef replied, 'Fried fish, sir.'

The captain's eyes boggled and he said, 'This is desecration – where did you learn to cook?'

He replied, 'Chatham Barracks, sir, this is how we were taught to cook fish.'

The captain, absolutely livid, said, 'I have news for you, my lad, you are on your way back to cookery school to learn how to cook fish in several different ways.'

The young officers' cook, within a couple of hours, was on his way back to Chatham Barracks to the cookery school still protesting loudly that everybody liked fried fish except that misery guts of a captain.

He was accompanied back to Chatham with a cryptic signal from our skipper describing this young man's culinary prowess and requesting that if this was the best they could do, they need not send a replacement chef. Needless to say, in a few days a new chef joined. (He must have been the pick of the litter. He kept the old man quiet and satisfied with his efforts.)

The Padre's Limousine 1942/43 Gibraltar

The 13th Destroyer Flotilla, of which I was a serving member as a young petty officer in an elderly destroyer (vintage 1916), had just arrived back in Gibraltar after long, arduous, dangerous, convoy trips lasting for some weeks. We had been away from England for one and a half years, and on the Rock of Gibraltar, our so-called base, there was no amusement whatsoever. A garrison of some seventy-five thousand servicemen of all denominations, and that was it. Despite our base being Gibraltar we served from Alexandria to Land's End, via South Africa.

Having arrived from our latest jaunt away, we tied up in Gibraltar, and soon our flotilla padre paid us a visit. We never saw him too often as we were always away on escort or convoy duty. The padre pulled up alongside the ship in his 1931/32 Morris Minor tourer, no hood. It was a most dilapidated-looking jalopy – bare of paint, rusty, a real heap. There had been no vehicle maintenance on Gibraltar since 1939 for civilian vehicles.

Our first lieutenant met him at the bottom of the ship's gangway and, in his usual, exuberant, forthright manner, told the padre what his means of conveyance on the Rock looked like. The padre's reaction was, 'How can I do anything about it? There are no facilities on the Rock for civilian vehicle-painting or maintenance.'

Our first lieutenant, like the rest of the crew, wanted something different from sea-going duty, watch-keeping, anti-aircraft, and sub duties etc.

The first lieutenant said to the padre, 'Leave your vehicle on the dockside at the bottom of our gangway, the ship's sentry will watch it and we will repair, paint and restore it.'

The padre accepted the offer and went on his way rejoicing, promising to return in some two days' time to collect his limousine.

The next morning, the first lieutenant summoned myself, petty officer, captain of the fo'c'sle, the front end of the ship. Also present was the captain of the top, the petty officer in charge of the middle portion of the ship, as was the petty officer in charge of the stern portion of the ship. We all wondered what the hell he wanted, standing alongside the padre's 'heap' with his three senior NCOs in attendance.

He soon outlined his plans: we three senior NCOs were to be in charge of the 'facelift' on the padre's limousine and he made it clear there was no holds barred. We could do what we liked with this wreck, regarding rejuvenating its looks.

(In the Royal Navy, all ships fell into three divisions – the front, or pointed end of the ship was the fo'c'sle division, universal colour red. The whole of that part of ship had all equipment, buckets, brooms, scrubbers, ropes, chisels, hammers, etc. painted red. The top division was white, the stern or quarterdeck division – blue).

The colour system was to prevent each division thieving each other's equipment. It was not a success, as devious methods were used to remove one marking and replace it with another. However, with the padre's jalopy, there was a truce. (The front of the car was to be vivid red, the doors on both sides in the middle were to be white and the rear end (shaped like a bee's bum) was to be blue.

The lads on the ship entered the spirit of the thing with gusto. After all, they were the painters, egged on by various ideas by their mates. The padre's dilapidated vehicle was soon transformed, brilliant red at the front, with scarlet bonnet, mudguards, wheels, etc. The front bumpers were transformed from rust bars to silver by the application of admiralty silver paint called Silverene, and the rear bumpers got the same treatment. The centre of the car (doors etc.) were painted white, and the ship's artist painted in the centre of the doors in full colour a church pennant fluttering in the breeze, as flown by all men-of-war whilst conducting a church service on board. The rear end of the car, or bee's bum, was painted dark blue.

To add a little class, the engine-room crew chipped in. We got them to remove the radiator cap, make a section of piping into a small ship's funnel, cut a thread on the bottom and screw it into the hole left by the radiator cap. The 6 to 8-inch funnel was then painted with our flotilla funnel markings (two vivid red rings and a single black ring) to enhance the effect. Two wires were then strung from the little funnel to the top of the windscreen corner, each side with small flags every six inches or so dangling. (The result was outrageous – it looked like a demobilised ice-cream stall.)

To cap all this, some of our arch scroungers, armed with duty-free fags, went to the local Gibraltar North End Airfield and returned with some two gallons plus of one hundred Octane Spitfire Aviation Spirit, which was unobtainable due to wartime restrictions. This was put in the parson's vehicle tank. The brakes of this jalopy were virtually non-existent due to lack of service and repair.

At the appointed hour the padre returned to collect his vehicle as arranged. All the ship's company were in position to witness the collection. The padre walked round the end of the dockside buildings and his face went white, his jaw dropped. Our first lieutenant went to meet him. He protested vigorously at the desecration of his car. The first lieutenant convinced him it looked better. He eventually drove it away, struggling to control it under the influence of Spitfire petrol. It was rumoured he went round the Rock twice before he could stop it.

We sailed on convoy duty the day following that on which the padre collected his rejuvenated car and we did not return for some three weeks to a month. On our return to Gibraltar dockyard, the padre appeared on the dockside with his jalopy and on coming up the gangway he looked as pleased as punch. The first lieutenant met him, expecting some parson's strong language regarding his car but he was nonplussed by the padre's reaction.

He said, 'It is jolly good, everywhere I go people recognise me by my vivid-coloured car, they stop, wave, and it is marvellous. I wouldn't part with it for the world.'

This was not our expected reaction.

Whodunnit

The year was 1939, it was September, and the Second World War had only been declared a couple of days when a Royal Navy warship not far from our Bermuda Naval Base stopped, on the High Seas, a large German cruise liner, under a strange flag. She was arrested, and a prize Royal Navy crew was put on board to supervise her voyage into Bermuda, and the Royal Naval Dockyard at Ireland Island.

At this time in September 1939, in Bermuda no mechanically driven vehicles were allowed on the roads. The only forms of transport allowed were horse and carriage, bicycles, and boats.

On the way into Bermuda dockyard, the Royal Navy prize crew had a good look around the ship, in its stores, cupboards, compartments, and it soon became evident that this vessel, on the outbreak of war, was to become a depot/supply ship for German U-boats in the Atlantic, but had slipped up by being captured.

On the way into Bermuda, like the pirates of old, the prize crew earmarked the German stores on board for future reference. They dare not strike too soon as the German crew were aware and watching.

In Bermuda, the German crew were escorted off the ship and made prisoners of war. Others were sent off by legal methods to various embassies etc. at about 6 p.m.

It was made known to the Royal Navy prize crew (now the ship was in their unfettered possession) that the local Royal Navy paymaster and his crew would descend on the vessel at 9 a.m. the following day and make an inventory of everything on board. The Royal Navy amateur pirates realised that if they were going to 'hook' anything it had to be before the paymaster and his crew arrived at 9 a.m. – in other words, during about a twelve-hour period. (Plenty of time for small acquisitions but not long for larger stores.)

One chief petty officer had spotted a small brown paper parcel in the German ship's storeroom some nine by six inches in measurement. During the period 9 p.m. – 6 a.m., this parcel, not very big, was spirited off the ship before the paymaster's arrival. Later information revealed that the parcel contained three hundred U-boat crew wristwatches. These were sold to various Royal Navy members in the fleet a short time afterwards for £10 each – no questions asked. (Not a bad little earner, £3,000 tax free in 1939.)

In the German cruise liner's stateroom was a huge full-size grand piano. The German crew who had been with the ship since it was built said it was so big it was absolutely impossible to get that piano into or out of the ship's stateroom by any means, including having it taken to pieces by experts and then reassembled outside. Even in pieces the various exits and entries from the stateroom would not allow the passage of the dismantled bits for assembly elsewhere. To get it into the stateroom the deck plates above it were removed, a large crane lowered the grand piano in and the deck plates were replaced and welded, and the piano was welded to the deck and bolted, to prevent it rolling about in rough weather on cruises.

Between the 9 p.m. arrival of the liner in Bermuda, and the 9 a.m. arrival of the paymaster Royal Navy to start his compilation of the inventory, the grand piano was stolen, and as far as I know it has never been seen again.

Any budding Agatha Christies got any suggestions as to how it was nicked?

Naval Culinary Efforts

During 1940 I was serving in an armed merchantman, seized from the French Navy as she was in Plymouth when France capitulated to the German forces; we needed everything that floated with guns on board to survive at sea, it was after Dunkirk and our backs were to the wall.

This was a vessel of some two thousand five hundred tons, built pre-war (probably before the First World War). She was a coal burner, one of the last in service, and conditions on board were basic. To describe them as primitive would be praising them. After all, we pre-war servicemen had been brought up the hard way so when we said conditions were primitive we meant it.

The galley (cookhouse) consisted of a large compartment in which was a huge range of cast-iron old-fashioned black lead stoves, coal-fired, as used by our grandmothers and mothers. We had one cook whose sole job was to cook. He did not prepare anything. All food taken to the galley had to be cleaned, peeled, chopped, oiled, seasoned, put in trays and dishes all ready to put into the cavernous ovens in this old-fashioned galley, whatever you took to him you got back, be it a sheep in a baking tin with the wool on. He only cooked what the small crew prepared. He was a most unhappy individual, the cook, was a Royal Navy regular, good at his job, and that was it. Ashore and off duty he was always in trouble. He would get drunk ashore and get arrested. Late back from shore leave, forgetting to come back at all sometimes, with a very fiery temper.

In big ships all food was bought, brought on board, prepared and cooked in the galley (general messing). In small ships you were allocated the money, you did the rest: buying, getting it on board, preparing it and getting it to the galley (canteen messing). (Each system had its snags and advantages.) In large or small ships you were stuck with whatever system the ship was allocated.

In this ship we had a mixed crew of newly joined (hostilities only) ratings. They had just been called up, and long-service experienced bodies had to show the others the ropes. On the mess deck were some sixteen men. Two men did cook's routine for twenty-four hours, then two more took over. Due to the mixed crew, we had an 'old hand' with a 'new hand' to guide him through the intricacies of preparing food, making it, and getting it to the galley with the least disturbance from the cook, who had a nasty temper if things went wrong.

On the day in question, the new boy had been guided through preparing our meat ration, making a Yorkshire pudding, cleaning spuds and getting it into the galley before 9 a.m. to meet with the ship's cook's approval. All this had been done, the two duty mess cooks washed all utensils and stowed them away.

At about 9 a.m., the older hand said to the younger newly called-up chap, with an evil glint in his eye, 'You have forgotten the dessert.'

He replied, 'What are we having then?'

The older man replied, 'Chinese wedding cake.' (Rice.)

The younger one said, 'How do you make that?'

The seasoned hand said, 'Get that big baking tin.'

The younger man did this, the tin was some eighteen inches by eighteen inches and four to five inches deep. The old hand got a big tin out of the mess cupboard marked 'Rice' and put it on the table next to the large baking tin. He then said, 'There you are, put the rice in the tin, and cover it with water mixed with Carnation milk [evaporated], with sugar.'

The perplexed younger man said, 'How much rice do I need?'

The old-timer said, 'You have the tin of rice there, now put your hands in and show me how much rice you can eat.'

The rookie put his oversize maulers in the tin and came up with some half a pound of rice granules. He said, 'I can manage this, I think.'

So the old-timer said, 'Well there are sixteen of us in the mess so you need sixteen times what you have got there.'

The rookie said, 'Seems reasonable,' plonked sixteen handfuls, some eight pounds of rice, in the dish, and stood back surveying his handiwork.

The seasoned veteran said, 'Right, now a full tin of Carnation milk on that lot, topped up to the top of the dish with water, add one pound of sugar to that and you are away.'

The rookie did this and surveyed the large dish brimming with milky water, and said, 'What now?'

The old-timer said, 'It has got to go to the galley, be careful how you carry it, don't spill any. When you get to the galley put it on the table if the cook is there, but if the cook is not there, do him a favour and put it in the hottest of the three ovens.'

The old-stager knew the cook went to the toilet and had a smoke and a read of a book for some thirty to forty minutes before returning to the cookhouse and starting the cooking of the crew's food, ready for about 1 to 2 p.m. dinner daily.

The rookie went to the galley; no cook was present, so he opened the ovens, found the hottest one, loaded his brimming dish of rice into it and left the galley.

The cook came back about three-quarters of an hour later and stood in the galley chatting to his cronies and having a smoke.

Just before he was ready to start cooking, at about 10.30 or 11 a.m., still chatting to his mates he noticed that one of the huge square cast-iron oven doors kept rattling, pushing forward against the handle, receding and pushing again. He thought, What the hell is doing that in an empty oven? (There was also a smell of burning.)

After a while he opened the large oven door and was almost engulfed by a tidal wave of black rice pudding. The inside of the oven was black with burned rice pudding, the floor of the galley was covered in brown rice pudding and, to put it mildly, the chef was not amused; in fact, he was intent on murdering the culprit who had desecrated his lovely ovens.

There was no escaping the cook's wrath; he knew where the culprit was with only about three different messes on the ship. The poor old rookie spent hours cleaning black rice pudding off the ovens, off the deck and elsewhere. He was not amused when his experienced cookery mate explained to him that it was supposed to be a joke.

Entente Cordiale Royal Navy-US Navy

In 1942 I was in the task force *en route* for the Allied invasion of North Africa, serving as a twenty-one-year-old Royal Navy petty officer in HMS *Wishart*. We mounted three 4.7-inch BL (Breech Loading) guns and some eight torpedoes, plus AA guns. Our complement of men was some one hundred and fifty. We were part of the 13th Destroyer Flotilla (usually based on Gibraltar, and known as the 'Gibraltar Defence Flotilla'). Our sphere of action over two years ranged from Alexandria in Egypt to Plymouth, England with some defence of Gibraltar.

We were in the portion of the task force set to invade Algiers, the French Naval Base and famous North African port. We arrived off the port of Algiers in the dark, and all the invasion craft and troops went in to attack. The *Wishart* was instructed to patrol the entrance to Algiers Bay and if any French warships 'broke out' of the harbour, or anything else, they were to be stopped, and if necessary sunk if they tried to escape to the open sea.

The invasion was well underway after two or three hours, and the Allied Forces were making 'good progress' according to reports. The morning was misty and a pall of smoke lay over the whole harbour area and Algiers Bay. We were closed up at action stations and had been for hours.

The tension of waiting for 'action' was worse than 'action' itself when it came. I was captain in command of 'B' gun on the *Wishart*, or the second gun from the front or bow of the vessel. We were suddenly alerted by our main control tower to come to the 'first state of readiness': another craft had been picked up on radar, approaching us from Algiers Harbour.

I brought my gun to the 'ready' state, fully loaded, crew 'on their toes', and we thought, Is this it? Nobody knew what sort of vessel it was: a smaller craft or 'something big enough to blow us off the face of the earth'. The adrenaline was running and we saw our masthead challenge lights flash their recognition signal towards the 'intruder'. We knew that in seconds we could be fighting to survive, unless something happened. Suddenly, out of the gloom, fog and bad visibility ahead we saw a succession of coloured lights flashed in answer to our challenge. It was one of our ships. Word went quickly round that it was HMS *Malcolm*, another World War I-built destroyer, withdrawing from the main invasion force, as she had been hit by a shell from a French shore battery and was retiring to 'lick her wounds', and make repairs.

After this episode we suddenly heard the main engines increase speed; we were heading away from Algiers Bay seawards and had been joined by our 'chummy ship' HMS *Velox*, another ancient destroyer of the 13th Flotilla.

We wondered what the devil was going on, heading away from Algiers at high speed, the two of us. Gradually the news filtered through. The task force commander had ordered our two destroyers to go to the aid of the USS *Thomas Stone*, a Liberty ship with the task force that had been torpedoed the night before *en route* to Algiers. She was heavily loaded with tanks, ammunition, landing craft, vehicles, troops (some one thousand five hundred) and the torpedo which had hit her demolished her propellers, rudder, etc. She could not steam, steer, move or anything. Why she was left overnight on her own in that state I cannot envisage. *Wishart* and *Velox* came up with the *Thomas Stone* a few hours later. She was wallowing all alone in the Mediterranean with no escort, or help. I still wonder why the hell the submarine that disabled her didn't finish her off with another torpedo – there was nothing to stop them whatsoever.

We came alongside her and by tannoy between the captains of the ships, we made known who we were, what we were there for and requested full cooperation. Our mission – detailed by the task force commander – was to tow the *Thomas Stone* with all its equipment to Algiers Harbour, some three hundred to four hundred miles away.

Bearing in mind that the USS *Thomas Stone* was some fifteen thousand tons, *Wishart* and *Velox*, the destroyers sent to help, were one thousand one hundred tons each and not equipped in any way to tow a ship of this size, a dead weight. Commander Scott, captain of the *Wishart*, prepared to take the *Thomas Stone* in tow, with HMS *Velox* circling us with her asdics underwater sub detector gear. This would have been useless if an enemy submarine had come upon us, we were sitting ducks for a good submarine attack, both the *Thomas Stone* and the *Wishart*.

Lieutenant Keddie, the *Wishart's* second-in-command, a very efficient officer from an old Essex family, and I were sent to the stern of the *Wishart* to attach the tow lines to the stricken *Thomas Stone*. We had no means whatsoever of pulling wires, ropes, chain cable, and anything for towing, on our stern. All pulling, heaving, struggling, was by manpower. We had a number of men on the stern to act as a tug-of-war team for ropes, cables, etc.

Our captain skilfully moved *Wishart's* stern as near as he dared to the bows (front end) of the *Thomas Stone*. The huge bow of the *Thomas Stone* towered over our stern like a skyscraper. An infantry landing craft from the stricken ship came over to take our biggest towing wire back to the *Thomas Stone*. It came alongside, the wire was lowered, a US sailor tied a rope to it and the landing craft returned to the ship. We paid out the heavy tow wire, with men holding it in check on our deck, like a tug-of-war team. Suddenly the knot tied by the US sailor in the landing craft 'melted' halfway back to his ship. The 'bogus knot' let the long heavy wire hawser drop straight down from the *Wishart's* stern.

With much cursing and swearing, my lads, encouraged by myself and Lt Keddie, handhauled it back on our deck, having warned our captain on the bridge not to start the main engines with a wire hawser dangling by our propellers which could have disabled the ship. After much swearing, all was returned to normal. Back came the US landing craft, down went the heavy wire hawser into the boat, and the same US sailor tied the knot in the rope to it, to take back to his ship. (No prizes for guessing what happened.) The US craft was halfway back to their ship, the 'US-tied' knot 'melted' and the heavy hawser dropped down straight, near our propellers again.

Our lads were disgusted at this blatant inefficiency of basic knot tying by the US sailor and on the landing craft returning for the third time to try to get the tow rope over to the USS *Thomas Stone*, Lt Keddie and I had a job to restrain our men and their remarks to the US sailors in the landing craft.

A tall leading seaman RN shouted down at the US sailor responsible for the 'melted knots', 'We have got boy scouts of twelve who can tie better knots than you, call yourself a bloody sailor.'

The US sailor yelled back, 'If I come up there I will knock your f— head off.'

My English wag replied, 'If you are as good at fighting as you are at knot-tying you will not last very long.'

We eventually got the tow line over to the *Thomas Stone* and started to tow her towards Algiers at some three knots. We realised it would be a long job, getting her to Algiers. (Our biggest tow wire was three inches in circumference. We had asked the USS *Thomas Stone* what her biggest tow wire was on board and had received the reply 'three inches' – the same as ours.)

The following day, creeping towards Algiers, a few men on deck with myself and Lt Keddie were remarking how much faster we could tow with a thicker tow rope. Out of the blue a voice from one of the crew said, 'The Yank has got a thicker tow rope than this one we are using.'

Lt Keddie in disgust shouted, 'We have asked the *Thomas Stone* if it has a thicker tow rope than ours at three inches. Her reply was that their "thickest tow" was a three inch rope.'

The voice then said, 'Ask the Yank how they measure wire rope, by the circumference or diameter?'

Lt Keddie was temporarily flummoxed but he went to the bridge of the *Wishart*, signals were exchanged and it turned out that their measurement was by diameter. A much thicker rope. The tow line was quickly changed and we towed the fifteen thousand ton ship to Algiers at six knots. I got hold of the character who told us of the different ways the Yanks measured wire ropes, and when I asked him how he knew this, he replied, 'Before the Navy called me up I was in the Merchant Navy and served on American ships.' (My reply I cannot reveal.)

During this very hazardous towing operation, every day the *Thomas Stone* sent us, by boat, fresh pork, bread, potatoes, oranges and goodies of all sorts. We hoped the tow would last forever. We had been on boiled rice, bully beef and hard biscuits for weeks. After some four days we towed the *Thomas Stone* into Algiers Harbour. She was then moored bow and stern and used as a depot ship.

The Yanks never forgot us. We operated along the North African Coast in support of the 1st and 8th Armies in the North African Campaign to expel Rommel and his German Army from North Africa. Every time we entered harbour in Algiers, usually short of all sorts of rations, a boat from the *Thomas Stone* appeared alongside the *Wishart* with fresh bread, meat, fruit etc., and we were most grateful, no other boat received this treatment.

Diplomacy

In the year 1938, I was a young seaman in one of His Majesty's cruisers of the South American Squadron Royal Navy, on a courtesy visit to Buenos Aires, Argentina. There were four of us young sailors in the local bar. It was crowded, we sat at our table with two spare chairs, drinking the local beer and talking of nothing in particular. We had all just been paid our residue of 2/– per day for one month (10p per day new money). We could only afford one splash ashore and this was it. (We would virtually be broke for the rest of the month except for the essential stamp money to write to Mum and other essentials that we had to save for.)

We glanced towards the door of the bar after a bit of a disturbance and saw two over-six-feet tall German officer cadets in the uniform of their mercantile marine, from a German cruise liner in the harbour (if I remember correctly the North German Lloyd merchant cruiser liners). They walked round the bar and, unable to find a seat, they approached our table and asked if we would mind them joining us at our table. Being in Royal Navy uniform, and knowing the tension regarding German aggression on other countries at the time, we were rather surprised (as there was a good chance of war between our two countries).

We invited them to sit at our table and they sat down with their drinks; they could both speak perfect English, were blonde, blue-eyed, they were the acme of German perfection, the Herrenvolk rulers of the world.

We chatted about things in general, keeping off politics, religion, race, etc. We all knew the pitfalls of these subjects and steered well clear of them, *except* – one of our party. He had not said much up to this time, but under the influence of his beer he said to the Germans, during a lull in the general conversation, 'Your country is a bit of a problem now to the rest of the world. Your leader Adolf Hitler is becoming a big pain in the arse to the rest of Europe, he always wants to be top dog, taking over this country and that, which doesn't belong to you anyway, and is proving to be a bit of a prat. What do you two think of this idiot and his tactics?'

There was a frozen silence at our table. We looked at our shipmate in horror, we thought, What now? A big punch-up because of this stupid berk. The German cadets, looking embarrassed, suddenly shot upright to attention, clicked their heels, nearly shaking down the building, gave the Hitler salute, yelled, 'Heil Hitler' and marched out of the bar in step.

The arch culprit sitting at the table looked at the rest of us and said, 'What was wrong with them? Did I say something wrong?'

We were speechless, we dragged him out of the bar and back to the ship before his diplomacy caused any more problems.

Mistaken Identity?
Mediterranean Fleet

In early to mid 1943, I was serving in an old destroyer, built in 1916, but a sturdy well-engined boat. Despite her age, the old girl could knock up thirty-three to thirty-four knots. We were escorting a merchant convoy along the North African coast to supply our famous 1st and 8th Armies converging on Cape Bon and working for the expulsion of Rommel from North Africa with his German forces.

The convoy was in some four columns, consisting of about thirty-five merchant ships, all experienced merchant crews that, with our losses of ships and merchantmen at that stage in the war, were worth their weight in gold. Our captain, a senior Royal Navy commander, a veteran of the First World War, was senior officer in charge of the Royal Navy convoy escort. It was a beautiful day, we were somewhere between Oran, the former French Naval Base, and Algiers; the Naval escort ships fussed around the convoy.

We proceeded eastwards, the sea was dead calm, no wind, blue sky, all was peaceful and serene. I was on deck near my 4.7 gun and crew. I was captain of the gun, we were the duty gun, it was about 3 p.m. and no alarm or signal had sounded. Suddenly there was a loud explosion, followed shortly by another. I looked in the direction of the sound of the explosions and saw that the two leading ships of the right-hand column had been hit by torpedoes and were sinking fast. I immediately switched my attention to the third and fourth ships in the right-hand column, expecting them to be hit next, but the crafty old convoy skippers, when they saw the leading ships hit, put their rudders hard over to starboard and turned out of the convoy line, towards the enemy submarine somewhere between the North African coast and the convoy, thereby presenting a head-on target to the submarine; they were not hit. The two stricken vessels were sinking fast and were soon out of sight below the waves. Ships of the escort and small boats, hastily lowered, recovered survivors. Soon calm was restored and the convoy sailed on. The anti-submarine vessels that scoured the area returned to their escort positions round the convoy.

Our captain signalled his second in command of the convoy escort to assume command and added, 'The submarine may be lying on the bottom after her attack. He must come up after dark to charge his batteries. I will sit on the area to welcome him when he does.' The convoy ploughed on eastwards and we criss-crossed the area where we thought the submarine would be, with asdics going all the time to detect any underwater movement.

I took over as NCO in charge of the duty 4.7 ship's gun with my crew at midnight, destined to stay there until 4 a.m., the much-disliked middle watch on ships. It was a beautiful Mediterranean night, moonlight, the sea like glass, and quiet. We were still crossing and re-crossing the area where our captain estimated the enemy submarine to be lying doggo. The duty gun crews were on their toes ready to go into action when required. The anti-submarine detector gear was pinging away for all to hear from the ship's bridge. All was quiet and under control.

Suddenly the bridge port look-out, a young able seaman, yelled, 'There the bastard is.'

The officer of the watch, a young lieutenant Royal Navy, shouted, 'Make a proper report, you bloody idiot.' (The look-out, very excited at his sighting had completely forgotten the correct method of informing the bridge crew of his sighting.)

Recovering his composure he yelled, 'Submarine on surface red forty-five degrees travelling from right to left.'

The officer of the watch shouted to the wheelhouse crew, 'Full speed ahead, hard to port.'

The ship slewed at full speed, heading for the submarine. We had flashed our masthead recognition lights at the vessel and had received no reply. The officer of the watch gave the order, 'Open fire.'

The two-pounder Pom Pom guns started to chatter as did the two 20 mm Oerlikon cannon guns on the sides of the bridge. Flashes and sparks flew off the submarine conning tower as she was hit; my 4.7-inch gun was loaded and I shouted to the gunlayer, 'Open fire' almost as the officer of the watch gave the order.

A blinding flash and a roar and my 4.7-inch shell was on its way, followed by another. The next thing we heard, the captain arrived on the bridge, the officer of the watch shouted over the front of the bridge, 'Stand by to ram' and we threw ourselves flat on the deck with our feet towards the bow of our ship (as practised in peacetime).

We could see we were within some seventy-five yards of the submarine when recognition lights flashed on the submarine. We were going at full speed, and I heard the captain yell to the helmsman, 'Hard a starboard, full speed astern,' but we all knew it was too late.

There was a heavy crash as we hit the submarine about halfway between the conning tower and the stern. There was a tearing, rending sound of metal on metal, we were embedded in the submarine and then bounced off.

Our captain was furious. He waited until the two stricken vessels were apart, switched on his loudhailer and yelled at the submarine, 'Who are you, and what are you doing in this area, you are not supposed to be here?'

The reply came, 'We are the French submarine —. We left Oran today to travel to Algiers.'

Our captain yelled back, 'Where is your escort?'

The French captain said, 'He was too slow for me so I left him behind and came on ahead, I want to get to Algiers.'

Our skipper yelled back, 'You are twelve miles ahead of your reported position at this time, and some fifteen miles further out to sea than you should be at this time.'

The French captain replied to the effect that he was aware of that.

Our captain drew near the stricken submarine, which was not in immediate danger of sinking, and said, 'Have you any casualties?' (Her upper deck had been raked with our gunfire.)

The reply came back, 'One French ensign [midshipman], the officer of watch on the conning tower, is seriously wounded, the helmsman is also wounded.'

Our captain said, 'I will send a boat over to collect your wounded to be treated by my ship's doctor. Perhaps you can see now the result of your actions.'

There was no reply. The ship's whaler was lowered and went alongside the French submarine to pick up the wounded ensign and able seaman. When we got them on board it was seen that the young French ensign had been hit in the middle of his back by a 20 mm Oerlikon shell, the able seaman in his right buttock by a 20 mm Oerlikon shell. The ensign died a few hours later, but the doctor patched up the able seaman and he was okay. We all thought what a waste of a young man's life due to his captain's stupidity. (Some blame must attach to the dead ensign and the wounded helmsman on the submarine conning tower, in charge of the boat, when they failed to answer our signal challenge as we went in to attack; a correct reply would have obviated any further action.)

We stayed with the stricken submarine until a tug came out from Oran and towed her back to the dockyard. After she had been rammed, her engines, rudders, etc. did not work.

Speculation was rife regarding our seriously damaged bows; we could not remain at sea in heavy weather, and rumours indicated we had to return to England for repairs after some two years away. We got a shock; our next orders were to go to Oran for repairs and we were put in the next dry dock to the French submarine we had almost sunk. Talk about friction, can you imagine what bunch of idiots thought up a solution like this? In the local bars and restaurants hostility arose between the crews; we had not exactly been in love with them before the encounter. You can imagine the situation afterwards. (A medal should have been awarded to somebody for diplomacy for arranging that venue for repairs.)

Some months later, a court martial was held in Gibraltar regarding this incident involving the French captain of the submarine and our destroyer captain, under Admiral of the Fleet, Sir Andrew Cunningham C in C. The French captain was held wholly and solely to blame for the fiasco and was suitably punished.

After the court martial, Sir Andrew Cunningham sent a personal signal to our ship's company which he had to word rather carefully; it was to the effect 'I congratulate you all on your very efficient action on the night of — when you encountered an Allied submarine in unforeseen circumstances. It was a great pity it was not an enemy submarine and I hope the next one you meet is a German.'

Acquisition of Stores

In 1942, at Gibraltar, I was a seaman petty officer on HMS *Wishart*. Our first lieutenant, an Essex man, was tall, young, athletic and very efficient. He would have had a very good career in the Navy and I think would have risen to high rank, but was unfortunately killed in action whilst commanding a Hunt class destroyer the following year, in the North Sea, still in his early twenties.

The day was bright and sunny. I was looking at our 20 mm Oerlikon anti-aircraft guns with the first lieutenant on deck. We had trouble with our Oerlikon gun ammunition magazines due to salt encrusting on them in an exposed position on deck, and the guns with their precision firing mechanism would jam when needed most. Oerlikon magazine storage lockers were in short supply and only fitted to larger, newer ships. The first lieutenant looked at our motley collection of magazines in their inadequate storage and said, 'I wish we had some watertight Oerlikon magazine lockers to keep these in good order.'

I said, 'Can't we "demand" two on store notes?'

He replied, 'It is hopeless we are an old destroyer, we would never get them. We are well down the list of ships to be supplied.' He then carried on with his walk of inspection round the upper deck.

Later that morning he returned from the dockyard, rather excitedly called me to one side and said, 'There is a new batch of Oerlikon lockers just delivered to the dockyard store.' He told me their exact location and where he had seen them in the store.

I said to him, 'What are you telling me this for, sir?'

He said, 'Look, you have several mobilised London ex-burglars in your division, how about taking a couple of chaps over to "get" a pair of lockers.'

I said, 'Do you mean that you want me to steal two Oerlikon lockers from the store?'

He said, good-humouredly, 'Oh, shut up, go on, get on with it. You are only re-distributing service stores from one place to another.'

I knew from experience, that at about twelve noon there would only be one storeman in the store, so I chose two of my Cockney seamen, who entered into the spirit of the thing, when I told them what we were to do. I had picked the right two.

We borrowed a large hand cart from the dockyard base and trundled it to the store. I went in with a 'demand' note for cotton waste and metal polish. Inside the main store doors to the right was a batch of new Oerlikon gun magazine lockers, labelled HMS *Nelson*, *Howe*, etc.

I went into the store as a decoy, and gave my demand stores note to the storeman who issued me with a bale of cotton waste and a box of tins of metal polish, after I had asked about other stores, and requested the storeman show me them. As I left the store I could see my two men careering up the dockyard road towards our ship with two Oerlikon lockers on the handcart. I dumped my stores for collection later, and took off after them, at high speed.

As we pulled up alongside the ship, I saw two civilian dockyard welders just taking their welding gear off our ship where they had been working, who could be so lucky? The lads carried the heavy steel lockers up the gangway and placed them on the deck near the Oerlikon guns.

I said to the welders, 'Forty cigarettes if you will weld them to the deck, where they are.'

They agreed instantly as cigarettes were in very short supply and in a few minutes the lockers were welded to the deck. The workers then left the ship with all their welding gear, and cigarettes.

I said to my two Cockney lads, 'Right, go up to the paint shop, get a pot of crab fat [Naval name for battleship grey paint] and paint those lockers as fast as you can; first get rid of that hand cart.' (Parked near our gangway.)

No sooner was this order carried out then I saw an irate paymaster lieutenant commander coming along the dockside with the Gibraltarian storeman from the store, who immediately identified me as being the only one to visit the stores, when the lockers were missed. (I was with him in the store all the time.)

The Paymaster Lieutenant Commander came on board and said to me, 'Where is your first lieutenant?'

I replied, 'I will fetch him, sir.'

I went to the Wardroom and told the first lieutenant he was wanted up on deck, re: Oerlikon lockers.

He followed me on deck. I watched his face as he stepped on deck and spotted the lockers, in place, welded down and painted. His jaw dropped and I thought he would give the game away; he then recovered and said to the paymaster, 'What is the trouble?'

The paymaster explained and the first lieutenant walked over to the lockers, kicked them and said, 'These are all we have. If you want to look round the ship help yourself.'

The Paymaster and the storeman looked round the upper deck and left the ship after an unsuccessful search, muttering all sorts of threats.

When they left, the first lieutenant said to me, 'How on earth did you do it?'

I grinned and he then said, 'Go down to the wardroom and get three bottles of beer for you and the lads, well done.'

Those lockers stood us in good stead in the battles that followed; our Oerlikon guns never jammed. The battles included the North African landings, support to 1st and 8th Army, two Malta convoys, invasion of Sicily, invasion of Italy and surrender of the Italian Grand Fleet at Taranto, Salerno and Anzio landings, etc.

Convoy Adventures

In 1941, during the Second World War, I was a twenty-year-old petty officer Royal Navy, having joined the Service in September, 1936, at HMS *Ganges*, Shotley, Ipswich, Suffolk, as a fifteen-year-old boy. In 1941, I was the bosun and chief gunnery rating of a flower class corvette. About two hundred of these small sturdy vessels were built by the Admiralty for convoy escort work. They were of some six hundred tons, based on the design of the Hull whaleback trawler, for fishing in the Arctic area, well tested by the fisherman of Hull and Grimsby pre-war whilst fishing in northern waters. These vessels were built up on the superstructure and carried a crew of some five to six officers and a crew of about one hundred men.

The usual fish decks and storage space was converted to crew's quarters, with bunks, tables, stools and other equipment, like magazines and shellrooms. These ships were rather primitive compared to larger, modern men-of-war. Serving in them was so bad that even in time of war you could request a transfer after nine months in one and get it. (Not many asked for a transfer as we are a sea-faring nation.) Fresh food, bread, vegetables ran out after a week. You were then on Spratts-type dog biscuits and corned beef for days on end. Cooking food (if you had any) was a hazard, as you could not keep pots and pans on the stove if you tried, with the ship rolling some forty-five degrees each side, jumping, twisting, and heaving. You could only eat something held tight in your hand, put it down on a table and it was gone. Our usual convoy run from Liverpool to Gibraltar and return took fourteen days each way or thereabouts. When the sea didn't hammer you, German submarines and aircraft took over the job. One convoy left Liverpool in September/October 1941 with twenty-eight merchant ships. Fourteen days later on arrival at Gibraltar we had fourteen left. This convoy was partly the subject of Nicholas Montsarrat's book, *The Cruel Sea*. He was a wartime officer in our escort group, I understand.

All these corvettes were named after species of flowers, and to be a regular Navy man, having served in crack naval ships, to be asked by old shipmates the name of your present ship and to reply *Poppy*, *Hollyhock*, *Tulip*, *Cowslip* etc. was nearly the excuse for a punch-up. These little escort ships were fitted with reciprocating engines capable only of some eighteen knots flat out. German U-boats could outrun us on the surface at twenty-six knots. The corvette's main gun on the fo'c'sle was a World War I four inch gun, a breech loader, slow firing. Most U-boats had two 4.7-inch quick firing modern guns on the surface, more than a match for a corvette.

In about October, 1941, I had managed to get a few days' leave between convoys; most of this leave was spent on railway trains between Liverpool and Norfolk. On my return to Albert Dock, Liverpool, my escort group base, I approached the ship with my attaché case in hand climbed the gangway and saw the ship's sentry (armed in wartime) hopping from foot to foot looking a bit agitated at seeing me. I also heard from the crew's quarters the sound of a 'knees-up' with loud music.

I put my case down and said to the duty sentry, 'What the hell is going on down there?' pointing to the duty crew's quarters.

Looking pale round the gills, he replied, 'There are two ladies down there, invited on board by the lads at lunch time.' (It was now about 3 p.m.)

I said to him, 'This is supposed to be a man-o-war, you are supposed to be guarding it, what are they doing on board?'

He made a non-committal reply.

I went down to the crew's quarters and told the two women there to lose no time in getting off the ship unless they wanted to be arrested. The elder of the two females remarked on her way up the ladder and off the ship, 'He is a miserable sod.' After they had left the ship I read the riot act to the crew members present. I told them in passing that they had not heard the last of the incident in more ways than one. I knew what they had been up to (I was later proved correct in my assumption).

We left Liverpool a couple of days later with a slow convoy of some thirty merchantmen (top speed about eight knots), bound for Gibraltar; the supplies they carried were for our hard-pressed Middle East forces in North Africa who were fighting Rommel.

The convoy headed well out into the Atlantic after rounding the North of Ireland to try to avoid the ever present U-boat packs. We were some eight days out from Liverpool. The sea was rough, but not excessively so. I was trying to have breakfast in the petty officers' mess when a knock came on the door.

I shouted, 'Come in.'

The door opened and a rather worried-looking able seaman put his head round the door and said, 'Can I have a word with you, Bosun?'

I said, 'Of course, come in,' indicating to the mess where several NCOs were eating.

He replied, 'No not here, somewhere on the quiet.'

I replied, 'Come with me,' got up and took him to a quiet compartment nearby and shut the door. I said, 'Now what is wrong?'

He replied, 'It is something down below,' pointing to the front of his trousers at the flies area.

I said, 'What is wrong down there?' (having a good idea what his problem was).

He replied, 'Each time I go for a pee I get pains down below.'

I said, 'Is it like broken bottles in your water pipes?'

He replied, 'Yes, how did you know?'

I said to him, 'In my early days in the Royal Navy I was serving in one of His Majesty's cruisers on a foreign station. I broke a bone in my hand, falling on deck one day, and with my forearm and hand in plaster I had to work in the sick bay instead of on deck for six to seven weeks. During this time I saw all the ship's unfortunate gentlemen who had caught VD on shore, having their treatment, and listened to their symptoms. I think you have got VD. Was this a result of the two ladies I found on the ship when I came back off leave unexpectedly in Liverpool?'

He replied sheepishly, 'Yes.'

I said, 'At the time I warned you that you and others had not heard the last of this incident.' He nodded and I said, 'See what I mean?'

He again nodded.

I said, 'Now, drop your trousers and pants.' This he did and I said, 'Now I want you to do a little test on your privates.' I instructed him how to do it and from what I saw I said to the able seaman 'You haven't got VD, it has got you. You require urgent medical treatment from a doctor, which we do not have.' I then said, 'Go and pack your kit and be ready at short notice to transfer to a ship in the convoy with a doctor.' We were still some seven days from Gibraltar and any medical help for this man.

I should explain that we only carried a sick berth attendant, well-known in Naval circles as a 'poultice walloper'; he was skilled at cut fingers, damaged legs, bruises, sprains and minor first aid. That was his lot – when he was not seasick. Our young man was prostrate as soon as he saw the open sea and if I and others had not forcibly fed him on the trip he would have died of starvation. He could not sit or stand at sea and was eventually transferred to the Army. I was sympathetic to him as I have been seasick and know the feeling.

I went up to the bridge of the ship and confronted the captain, a lieutenant commander RNR, a peacetime Merchant Navy officer who appeared (and was) semi-permanently under the influence of alcohol day and night. I went up to him, saluted and said, 'Captain, sir, we have a bit of a problem, there is an able seaman below who, in my opinion, is suffering from acute VD and requires rather urgent medical attention.'

After a pause, looking at me through an alcoholic haze, he said, 'How did he get that?'

I replied, 'The usual way, sir.'

The captain then said, 'Does he realise how awkward it is to deal with this sort of thing in the middle of convoy duty?'

I made non-committal remarks and survived his stupid chatter and managed to get him to signal our flotilla leader at the head of the convoy (which carried a doctor), informing them of the situation. Almost immediately the reply came back, 'Transfer this man to me for urgent medical help.'

The captain waved the signal sheet under my nose to read and in a slurred voice said, 'Now you have got to get him over to the flotilla leader.'

I said, 'Me, sir?'

He said, 'Yes, you. Put him in a lifeboat and row him over to the group leader.'

I said to the captain, 'I am the bosun of this ship, sir. We have leading seaman who are the normal coxswains of these boats – it is not my job to do this.'

The captain said, 'You are more experienced than them in boat handling, you take the lifeboat over.'

I said, 'How do you expect these men to gain experience if you will not let them do the job?'

He replied, 'Get on with it, that is an order.'

I went down to the ship's starboard lifeboat, and handpicked my crew of five oarsmen. I got my VD victim in the boat with his kit and when it was ready lowered it towards the rough water below. I had the crew ready as far as possible, 'oars in rowlocks'. My right hand was poised over the automatic dropping gear lever; when this was hit by the coxswain's hand the boat and crew dropped like a stone. You had to get the drop right by landing on top of a passing wave, a small drop; if you went down into a trough you could fall ten to fifteen feet and on hitting the water the crew's buttocks would finish up under their hats. I hit it just right, a small drop, and I yelled at the crew to 'Row like hell,' as I steered the boat away from our ship into open water towards our flotilla leader.

I steered the boat towards the flotilla leader and eventually drew alongside her; we were heaving up and down in the rough choppy sea. Ropes were thrown to us and we were pulled alongside her. We quickly transferred our shipmate and his kit as we were heaving up and down alongside the flotilla leader, one minute almost level with her propellers (threshing alongside our boat), and in a few seconds level almost with her upper deck. I was glad when I steered the boat away from her and got into open water and ordered the crew to row towards our corvette.

I lined the boat up on a course to bring us alongside and to hook on to the boat's falls (ropes/blocks) to be hoisted on board. The captain, in his present state of intoxication, headed the ship into the sea and waves were rolling down the ship's side as it slowed down. I made one attempt to hook on but it was too dangerous. I steered the boat into open water near the ship as close as I dared. I stood up in the stern of the lifeboat, cupped my hands to my mouth and yelled at our captain, 'Turn the bloody ship in a tight circle to smooth the water whilst we come and hook on.' The captain did this and I took the boat alongside under the davits and hooked on in minutes; we were soon hoisted on board.

When I had secured the boat and made sure the boat's crew were all right, I heard a yelling from the bridge for the bosun to report to the captain at once. I went to the bridge, drew up in front of the captain and said, 'You sent for me, sir?'

He then told me in real sailor's language that he did not need me to tell him how to handle his ship.

I replied, 'You did not give me any help in rough water to get the lifeboat alongside and hoist it. I was concerned for the safety of myself and the lifeboat crew, hence my angry reaction.'

He replied, 'Get off the bridge, I will deal with you later, get ready for a court martial when we reach Gibraltar for your conduct today.'

(We heard from the flotilla leader, later, shortly after we returned to normal, that the man we had transferred shortly before had been examined by the ship's doctor, he was suffering from VD and did require urgent medical treatment. I saw the signal sent to our ship. I asked the captain whether he thought my diagnosis was reasonable and the reply was unprintable.)

Our convoy pressed on towards Gibraltar and we were shortly detailed by the senior officer of the escort to take over the duty of stern sweep to protect the rear end of the convoy from submarine and aircraft attack; these used to sneak up astern and despite radar and asdics were somehow missed, with disastrous results.

This convoy was the first to be accompanied by a new pocket aircraft carrier, a large merchant ship, fitted with a flight deck capable of handling fighter planes and equipped with six Grumman Martlet American-built fighter planes, crewed by our Fleet Air Arm pilots. We had welcomed this additional resource to the convoy defence to combat the large German Focke-Wulf four-engined bombers, flying out from the French Brittany coast to attack our Atlantic convoys, mainly on the last run in to Gibraltar. These large aircraft were coordinated to attack our convoys in conjunction with the U-boat packs of submarines. (One day you would be attacked by U-boats, the next day Focke-

Wulf bombers, followed by U-boats, etc., but some days if the weather was right you received both.)

We were still stern sweep of the convoy, guarding the rear, some four days out of Gibraltar, and we criss-crossed the trail of the convoy with radar and asdics in operation. We had had a reasonable voyage, no persistent U-boat attacks or bombing. It was a lovely day, blue sky, calm sea, we were at peace with the world despite the war.

I was carrying out my ship's guns inspection and maintenance routine at about 12.15 p.m., as I was in charge of the ship's guns. I had almost completed my daily routine and had arrived on the rearmost anti-aircraft gun platform, one of the Royal Navy's famous two-pounder Pom Pom guns position.

I was checking the base of the gun and the rollers it revolved on. (We did not carry any ordnance staff to maintain guns in corvettes; you either did it yourself or stood the chance of something going radically wrong at a crucial time.) Where I was sitting on the deck, behind the gun, I was surrounded by a four-feet-high splinter shield, built to protect the gun crew from flying shrapnel from near misses. As I arrived on the gun deck I had spoken to a young ordinary seaman who was stern look-out, in contact with the ship's bridge by telephone if required. I had passed the time of day with him as I arrived at the gun platform and told him to keep his eyes peeled for trouble, air or surface wise as we had so far had a trouble-free trip from the enemy which was too good to be true.

During my check of the gun, still sitting on the deck, I heard the young look-out say to me rather nonchalantly, 'Look at this, here comes a Wellington, what about that?' (No air raid alarm had been received from the convoy and all was quiet.)

A few seconds later, I thought, Wellington bomber here, not likely. I stuck my head over the splinter shield in the direction the young look-out was looking in, and saw a four-engined German Focke-Wulf bomber at about three thousand feet, hell-bent on a bombing run at the bigger ships of the convoy, probably the carrier. I yelled at the look-out in real Naval bad language, telling him what I thought of his aircraft recognition, and told him to man the gun with me. I swung it round, drew a bead on it in my gun-sight and fired. The gun fired one shell and jammed, I re-cocked etc. but it would not clear. I was almost in tears to have this bomber in my sights and the gun jammed. However the shot I had fired alerted the convoy and all the duty guns on the Royal Navy and merchant ships also opened up. Still, no air raid alarm had been given to the convoy till I fired. The fighters on the carrier were scrambled, they shot the bomber down, and on patrol round, the convoy got three or four more waiting to attack.

I was quite pleased to have raised the alarm, although angry that my gun had jammed. After the attack had been dealt with, I was sent for by the captain to report to him on the bridge. He looked at me when I arrived through his usual alcoholic haze and demanded to know why I only fired one shell at the enemy plane.

I said to him, 'Well the gun jammed and we could not clear it in time to carry on firing.'

He then said, 'Why did the gun jam?'

I replied, 'I do not know at this stage, there are several reasons for a gun jamming.'

He leered at me and said, 'I will tell you why it jammed. It was sheer bloody inefficiency on your part, and another reason for me to get you court martialled on arrival in Gibraltar.'

I replied, 'That is your privilege, sir,' and left the bridge.

(No mention of me raising the alarm to the convoy, or of the destruction of the enemy aircraft and an unscathed convoy as a result of this.) The German crews in the bombers must have got a bit of a shock to be met by carrier-borne fighters so far out to sea with a normal convoy.

A few days later we all arrived safely at Gibraltar. On arrival, the escort group's gunnery officer came on board; he was based on Gibraltar and was responsible for all ships in our group gunnery-wise, i.e. repairs to weapons, supply of additional and new weapons, maintenance of guns and ammunition etc. He contacted me as usual and asked me about any difficulties with guns or ammunition on the convoy trip we had just completed. I informed him of the way the Pom Pom gun had jammed when I fired it at the enemy aircraft and his reaction was, 'It could happen to anybody.' I informed him of the captain's promise to court martial me in Gibraltar over the incident and he asked to see the gun and ammunition.

I accompanied him to the gun and told him I had done nothing to it except clear and oil it since the incident. He tested it as far as possible and said, 'As usual, your guns are well-maintained, I cannot fault them. I am now going to see your captain re his complaint and threat of court martial.'

Some time later he returned to me and said, 'I have spoken to your captain about the incident and his threat to court martial you and he told me he did not know what I was talking about. But I told him that if he carried out his threat I would attend and give evidence on your behalf regarding the state of the guns on my various inspections.'

I thanked him and he left the ship.

It was ironic that a few weeks afterwards I was mixed up in a court martial; it was that of my captain. (This, of course, is another story.)

Dunkirk Adventure
(Royal Navy Style)

It was May or June 1940, the Dunkirk evacuation was in full swing, the Royal Navy, with all sorts of craft, were working overtime to save as many men from the Dunkirk beaches as possible. An old shipmate of mine (who told me the story verbatim) was serving as an able seaman in one of His Majesty's destroyers HMS *Grenade*, a reasonably modern craft. During the mêlée off the beaches, this destroyer struck a German mine and sunk. My friend started swimming away from his sinking boat with other survivors and they were picked up by one of the old Eagle Paddle steamers which plied on the Thames, pre-war, with passengers. Thankful to be out of the water, he dealt with his minor wounds, and shortly afterwards this craft was sunk by a German Stuka dive bomber. He started to swim again, rather fed up.

Shortly after this, he was picked up again by the old Great Yarmouth, Norfolk, wooden-built herring drifter, the *Polly Johnson*. (We were both Great Yarmouth boys and had been brought up with these old boats, many members of the family being fishermen who had served in them.) He had not been on board her long before a Stuka sunk her; he started to swim again, having gathered a few more wounds, one rather badly to his leg.

Not long afterwards, he was picked up by another old pleasure boat which came to the rescue. In a short while she was also sunk by German aircraft and he took to the water again. He was rescued by a fifth ship and in a matter of hours she was sunk under him as well by German aircraft. In just over twenty-four to thirty-six hours he had five ships sunk under him and he decided enough was enough. His lifebelt inflated, he decided to stay in the water. A large piece of wooden wreckage floated nearby so he clung to this and when ready he hauled himself on it. The Dunkirk evacuation was in its closing stages and as night fell, that day, he dozed off, exhausted. The weather was reasonably calm and he slept most of the night.

He woke up the next morning; it was fine and a bit sunny, he lifted his head and had a quick look round, nothing in sight except sea, no land, nothing. He went to doze off again when he heard a shout. He got up on his elbows, rubbed his eyes, and looked round again. About five yards away behind him was a ship's rowing lifeboat from some sunken craft, with three British soldiers in it, rowing the boat. One of the soldiers called to him, 'You look like a Naval man,' looking at the tattered remains of his uniform.

He replied, 'I am, so what?'

The soldier spokesman then said, 'Will you come into the boat and show us the way home, we cannot navigate, we don't even know where we are.'

My old shipmate did not let on, but muttered, 'I don't bloody well know either.'

They rowed over to the wreckage he was laid on, and they helped him into the boat. After basic introductions he got the three soldiers rowing and he took the rudder. (When he told the story to me I ribbed him and said, 'They didn't fall for that one, them rowing, you resting.' He replied, 'P— off.') He went on to explain that when the sun was in the East in the morning he rowed, or his crew did, and he steered the boat away from it. They rested about twelve noon and in the afternoon when the sun went down in the West, he kept it in front of him. Four and a half days after the Dunkirk evacuation ended they were washed up on Ramsgate beach, in Kent. The coastguard and military found them all unconscious in the bottom of the boat, and removed them to hospital.

When cleaned up and rested, his wounds dressed temporarily, the hospital doctors saw him, and his soldier crew, and stated they could not stay there as all hospitals in South East England were full to the brim with Dunkirk casualties and they would be taken to their home hospitals by Army ambulance. This was done and my old shipmate finished up in Great Yarmouth General Hospital. He was cleaned up again, his wounds tended, and shrapnel removed from places which had not been dealt with before. After some twenty-four hours he was worrying the doctors to allow him to go home in the town. They decided to allow him out to go home. He left the hospital, complete with bandage turban for his head wounds, legs bandaged etc., and on borrowed crutches. Dropped near his home by transport (he did not want to alarm his mother by his appearance), he turned into the road he lived in on his crutches. On rounding a corner, hobbling home, he saw his fiancée, on the opposite side of the road, coming towards him on the arm of a Grenadier or Coldstream guardsman. He went berserk and shouted at her, 'That's right don't even let me get bloody cold before you look for somebody else,' waving his crutches in the air. (This was the end of a beautiful friendship.)

He made his way home, absolutely furious, and on going up the garden path to his house, he banged on the front door and it opened, his mother stood there, and he said, 'Hello, Mum.'

She let out a shriek, and fainted. One of his male relatives was in the house; he stood over his prostrate mum and said, 'What is wrong with her?'

The reply was, 'You silly bugger, she got a telegram from the Admiralty about a week ago saying you were "Missing Presumed Dead" when your boat was sunk. Now you turn up here looking like a bloody Egyptian mummy, what do you expect?'

After an hour or so, with loads of tea, etc., Mum recovered, and was delighted to get him back. He explained that he had not known about the telegram.

That night, despite warnings from the hospital doctors to take things easy, complete with crutches, bandages etc. he went to the local labour club and by accident or design he got drunk. About midnight he was flat out on the pavement in the main street, bandages all loose everywhere, crutches nearby, and the locals called the ambulance service (not the police) to get him home. Sympathetic towards a wounded serviceman, he was scooped up and taken home.

A few days later, he received a bill for 3/6d (old money) for use of the ambulance from the authorities. He went up to their office and played up hell about a wounded war hero being charged for this service etc.

A stony-faced fellow listened to his complaint and then told him, 'We run the ambulances for general public emergencies, not as taxis for drunken bloody sailors on Saturday nights. Now pay up or else.'

Rather disgruntled, he paid up, but was still complaining. In about a month he was back at sea on Royal Naval duties.

Etiquette (RN Style)

In about 1948, I was serving in a new, large, Home Fleet destroyer; we were in dry dock at Chatham, Kent, for routine servicing and repairs. I was a petty officer, duty NCO, and responsible for the running of the ship, under the duty officer, a lieutenant RN, South African by birth, and a good officer. When the crew were settled for the night and all quarters clean, at 9 p.m., I reported to the duty officer that the ship was ready for inspection. On completion of his round of inspection, the duty lieutenant said to me, 'Would you like to come to the wardroom (officers' mess) for a beer?'

I replied, 'Yes, sir, I would be glad to.'

We went to the wardroom, no other officers were on board, and I had a beer poured for me by the officers' steward and sat chatting with the duty lieutenant.

Suddenly the door opened and the ship's first lieutenant, the ship's second-in-command, walked in. He glared at me and said to the duty lieutenant, 'What is he doing here?'

The duty lieutenant replied, 'He is my guest, I invited him for a beer.'

The first lieutenant said to me, 'Put your glass down and get out.'

I replied, 'Yes, sir,' then carried out his order.

I was most embarrassed and could not understand the first lieutenant's reaction. There was a wide gulf between the officers and NCOs but an invite was an invite to join the officer in a drink. I was very angry at this unnecessary rebuff.

Some six months later, the ship laid in Portland Harbour and the Home Fleet Rowing Regatta was on. This was something like a Naval Newmarket races. All ships' boats that were racing were backed on like racehorses, and amateur bookmakers were operating in the fleet; lots of money was changing hands, and officers and men were both involved. (A tradition.)

For our ship I was the stroke oar of the chief and petty officers' racing whaler's crew, a twenty-seven foot long wooden boat with a crew of six. The one mile race, 'against the book' was won by my crew; the celebration was magnificent.

The next day, one of the officers, the engineer commander, the stroke oar of the officers' racing whaler's crew, fell down a ship's ladder, breaking his arm, and was unfit to row in the officers' final race, the following day. They had done well in the qualifying heats.

The ship's captain, a very senior commander, who had recently joined the ship, and who was in the officers' whaler's crew, as was 'my friend' the first lieutenant, approached me, saying, 'If I can get permission from the Regatta Committee, will you row in the officers' whaler's crew as stroke oar, we have nobody else available.'

I replied, 'Yes, sir, I will be pleased to help you out.'

He returned a short time later and said he had obtained official permission for me to row in the officers' crew.

The great day dawned and we lined up in Portland Harbour for the final one-mile race of the officers' whaler's crews. The gun went off and away we went. I started off at about 30 oar strokes a minute and gradually worked up to

36 strokes towards the end of the race. (The officers had a very good crew and I feel they would have won without me, normally.) We swept the board and were first by several lengths. The captain was delighted. (A lot of cash changed hands.)

On return to the ship, the captain said to me, 'Jolly good show, come to the wardroom to celebrate our victory.'

I replied, 'No thank you, sir.'

He said, looking very surprised, 'What the hell is wrong with you?'

I replied, 'I would rather not discuss it, sir.'

He smelled a rat. The first lieutenant was standing by us, as was the South African lieutenant, two members of the officers' racing whaler crew.

He said, 'I demand an explanation, Smith, this is not like you.'

I replied, 'On a previous occasion, sir, one of your officers invited me into your wardroom for a drink. Another officer entered the wardroom and ordered me out, before I had finished my drink, and, in my opinion, insulted me. I do not wish to go through that again.'

A very embarrassed-looking first lieutenant was standing nearby.

The captain was furious and immediately ordered all officers to the wardroom. After I had bathed and changed my clothes, a messenger came to the C&POs' mess and said, 'The captain wishes to see you in the wardroom.'

I went to the wardroom after some persuasion and had a celebration drink with the officers. The captain said, 'You will not be ordered out of the wardroom after an invite again.'

A very sheepish first lieutenant made it clear (on the quiet) that he had been officially instructed to apologise for his 'ungentlemanly' conduct on a previous occasion, 'or else'. Being a dyed-in-the-wool pre-war Naval officer this was what I expected. We all parted the best of friends, shortly afterwards. There was no doubt in my mind that in the 'post mortem', held by the captain, in the wardroom after the race, that somebody had received the mother and father of all bollockings. There are no prizes for guessing who got it.

Fishing?

It was 1942, and I was a young petty officer RN serving in a Med Fleet destroyer based on Gibraltar. We had just been on a long arduous convoy escort to Bathurst, West Africa, returning with two slow convoys, which had lasted some fourteen plus days. We came in to berth in the destroyer pens at the north end of Gibraltar Harbour. Our skipper, a senior commander RN (First World War vintage), had been in charge of the convoy escort for the duration of the convoy and had rarely left the bridge *en voyage*; he looked really exhausted. He brought the ship into harbour and, having got her near the destroyer berths, he called to the young first lieutenant on the side of the bridge, 'Take over and take her alongside, number one.'

The first lieutenant replied, 'Aye aye, sir.' And as the weary captain left the bridge to go to his cabin and sleep, he expertly brought the ship into its berth, alongside a concrete wharf, and made her secure, bow and stern.

After the ship had tied up, which was part of my job, I went along the ship's upper deck and, getting near the stern, I looked over the side into the water between the ship and the concrete wharf. There I saw a wooden catamaran floating between the wharf and the ship to keep the ship clear of the concrete wharf and any damage she could suffer if she touched it. In the water between the wharf and the ship, feeding on the seaweed on the wharfside, was a large shoal of sea bream, all silver and black, sleek and fat, about 2 lb. to 3 lb. each.

My eyes lit up and, having been a keen sea fisherman, boat, line and net, since an early age, I recognised a good fish supper when I saw it.

On this convoy duty we had run out of fresh meat, fresh bread, and fresh vegetables about a week before and had been living on boiled rice, corned beef, hard-tack biscuits (supplied by Spratts dog food manufacturers in 7 lb. tins). The sight of the fish shoal alongside the ship made my mouth water. The problem was how to catch them.

I quickly went to the ship's store where I knew there was some stale bread, and grabbed a loaf. I shouted to one of my petty officer colleagues nearby, who was NCO in charge of depth charges, 'Bring a small depth charge, some cable and a battery to the port quarter – we are going fishing.'

He was rather perplexed but arrived shortly afterwards with the gear. I was at this time sprinkling lumps of stale bread near the bream, alongside the ship, and they were feeding and gathering round the bread in dozens.

I took the small depth charge, fitted wires to it, lowered it down the side of the ship, and with the aid of a broom handle, to the end of which I tied the electric wires leading to the charge, I pushed it out from the ship side so it hung midway between the ship's side and the concrete wharf, a distance of some six feet. I did not want to blow a hole in the ship's side. I sprinkled more bread round the charge some three to four feet below the water and the bream began swimming thickly round the submerged charge.

My colleague, the depth charge expert, had connected the wire from the charge to a battery, except for the firing wire which he held poised over the battery terminal to fire the charge. When all was ready, more bread was dropped near the charge, more fish came and I called to him, 'Stand by.' When the fish were round the charge I called out, 'Fire.' He put the firing wire on the battery terminal and there was a huge bang alongside the ship; it shuddered and rocked at its moorings. When I looked in the water between the ship and the wharf it was thick with dead and stunned fish. (I had forgotten the charge was in a rather confined space, between the ship and wharf, hence the big bang and the ship rocking.)

I grabbed my landing net and started to scoop the fish into iron buckets near me on the deck. I was on my hands and knees having a whale of a time scooping fish out of the water into the buckets, thinking of fried fish, when I heard an angry shout from behind me saying, 'Petty Officer Smith, what the hell are you doing there?'

I glanced behind me and saw an irate commanding officer in his pyjamas and dressing gown, absolutely livid. I dropped the landing net, sprang to attention and saluted. I then said, 'I am fishing, sir,' pointing to the buckets of fish.

He said, 'I have been a fisherman all my life and I have never ever made as much bloody noise as you.' (He referred of course to the explosion when the charge went off, minutes before.) He then shouted at me, 'You nearly blew me out of my bloody bunk with that explosion; I was sound asleep and wondered what the hell had happened!'

I glanced down from where we were standing and with a quick calculation, I judged the charge must have been about 4 to 5 feet from the skipper's head when it detonated. I had forgotten about him asleep in his cabin, with only $3/8^{th}$ inch of steel plate of the ship's side and water between him and the charge going off. As he turned to walk back to his cabin, the old man turned and said to me, 'You make sure that some of those fish appear on the wardroom table [officers' mess] for my dinner, or I might change my mind and put you on a charge, do you understand?'

I saluted and said 'Yes, sir,' and he departed with a grin on his face, to get on with his disturbed slumbers.

Needless to say he got his good ration of fish and no more was said. I had enough fish in seven buckets to supply all the crew's fish eaters.

Fresh Bread

1941 at Albert Dock, Liverpool, my convoy escort group of flower class corvettes were tied up at their moorings getting ready for a slow convoy trip to Gibraltar. This took some fourteen days there, and after a few days in Gibraltar (if you were lucky) to refuel, carry out repairs, and stock up with victuals, ammunition etc., it was then fourteen days or more on the return trip to Liverpool, hammered most of the way by U-boats and long-range bombers from the French Brittany coast occupied by the Germans.

On convoy duty, after about seven days at sea, all fresh bread was gone, fresh meat, fresh vegetables, all exhausted. (You finished up eating Spratts biscuits (dog variety) supplied in 7 lb. sealed tins. Refrigerators or any similar unit could not find space (or perhaps be included in the cost of building these vessels).

As we lay in Albert Dock, Liverpool, I was on deck as duty NCO doing various checks and jobs when I saw a Naval character pushing a handcart along the dockside near the ship. He came up the gangway and said, 'Are you the duty NCO?'

I replied, 'Yes.'

He said, 'I have to report to you to join the ship.'

I looked at this man, who was in the uniform of a ship's cook, denoted by his sleeve badges. I was a twenty-year-old NCO with five years' service under my belt and I smelled something peculiar with this ship's cook. He was somewhere near the Royal Navy retiring age of forty years, having served twenty-two years, and was thus approaching pensionable service. The war delayed or stopped anybody leaving on pension, but this one was unusual.

I said to him, 'Are you a regular Navy man, a long service rating?'

He replied, 'Yes.'

I examined his papers, which did not reveal much except his official number, his rank, date of birth, date of joining the ship etc. I said to him, 'Never mind the bullshit – at your age, experience etc. as a regular, why are you still a low-ranking hash slinger?' (cook in Royal Navy slang).

He smiled and said, 'In my last ship, HMS — [battleship] I was a chief petty officer cook in charge of all the cooking facilities on board, but my love of the booze led to my demise. I missed the ship sailing a couple of times on shore leave, I got drunk on board on rum, I forgot to come back off long leave and I was busted from a CPO cook to the lowest grade; I lost my good conduct badges, and I am now the lowest form of animal life in the Royal Navy cooks' world.'

I listened to his story and took a shine to this character. I told him 'You must still be a good cook, that is what we need, keep your nose clean and dish up what you can with our limited supplies and I will not ruffle your feathers if the officers and crew are happy with their rations.'

This man was superb. No matter what the limited rations were, he transformed them: bully beef, burgers (hot), tinned sausage (hot). He had made the delicious fresh rations last longer, some nine to ten days, by good cooking. The crew reacted accordingly and were very satisfied with their new cook. (No fresh bread was a standing complaint from officers and men; it was marvellous what one could do with cooked bully beef if you had bread.)

I was in the galley (cookhouse) one day with our new ship's cook. I said to him, 'What a pity we cannot have fresh bread on this long voyage to and from Gibraltar each month. We have the flour, the salt, the other ingredients but we do not have yeast.'

The ship's old cook, looked at me and smirked. He said, 'What difference does that make?'

I sat up and took notice. I said, 'What do you mean by that remark?'

He replied, 'We have all the ingredients on this ship now for me to make all the crew fresh bread every day of the week.'

I sat and thought this over, thinking, What is this crafty old bugger up to? Then I said to him, 'What do you use for yeast?'

He replied, 'Stout. You get me four bottles (pints) of Mackesons stout from the officers' mess and I will make you some of the finest bread you have ever tasted, enough for the whole crew.'

I said to him, 'If you are pulling my leg I will have your guts for garters.'

He laughed and said, 'Test me, get the beer.'

This was so important an issue I dared not turn it down; what with the officers and crew for days on dog biscuits, it would be a miracle.

I went to see the captain at about 10 a.m. and explained the situation, and even in his usual intoxicated state he said, 'Get four bottles of Mackesons stout from the officers' steward and see what this so-called cook comes up with.'

I obtained the stout from the officers' steward, and took it to the galley (cookhouse) where the cook was waiting. He grinned at me as I went in there and he locked the door. I turned round with the beer bottles in my hands and was horrified to see two clean half-pint glasses lined up on the bench in the galley next to the bread-mixing bin. I said to the cook, 'What the hell are those two glasses for?'

He said, 'One bottle for me, one for you, and two for the bread.'

I said, 'Look here, I have stuck my neck out for you regarding fresh bread, if the captain and crew do not get hot fresh bread by about 5 p.m. there will be trouble, and lots of it.'

He replied, 'Relax, I knew I could make enough bread for the crew from two bottles of stout. This way they are happy, and you and I get a bottle each every day, and life will be easier.'

I said, 'Make sure the bread is good.' I stayed with him whilst he mixed it and put the two bottles of Mackesons stout in, mixed the dough, and waited until it had risen and was in the oven. It looked very nice. We each had our bottle of beer and at about 5 p.m. I went to the galley, not long after which the cook produced the most beautiful batch of bread, all hot, soft, and only slightly brown (the stout). The slight tang of beer did not bother the crew. I took the first four or five loaves to the wardroom (officers' mess) where they were waiting (except those on watch on the bridge). We took them slices of hot bread with all sorts of jam, marmalade, and corned beef on it along with butter and margarine, and everybody was delighted, the crew were almost doing handstands. The captain sent for me and told me to congratulate the cook and to collect four bottles of duty-free stout from the wardroom daily to keep up the fresh bread supply. The cook and I had our daily rendezvous with four bottles of stout in the cookhouse, one for him, one for me and two for the fresh bread. We had started a nice little harmless racket, everybody benefited and a hard life was made easier for everybody. The crunch was that we only enjoyed our little subterfuge for a few days before it was all ended; we had expected to do this regularly on convoy, but fate decreed otherwise. At the end of this convoy the ship was sent on a mission, we were shipwrecked and had to leave the badly damaged boat in Gibraltar dockyard whilst the crew were distributed as spares throughout the Med Fleet.

Another quirk to this story was that on arrival in Gibraltar, when the crews of the other boats in the escort group heard of how our crew had enjoyed fresh baked bread for some seven days after the Liverpool bread ran out, they went back to their ships and demanded to know why they couldn't have fresh bread daily made with beer. (Their young cooks did not have the know-how to produce it.) Things got a bit naughty on the return trip, which we were not on, regarding fresh bread.

We left Liverpool, saying goodbye to relatives and promising to return in about a month (with extra ration supplies from Gibraltar), and it was almost a year and a half before some of us got back, and then only briefly, before we returned to the Mediterranean within days.

How Lucky He Had Biscuits

It was the latter end of 1942, the Allies were preparing to invade North Africa at Casablanca, Oran, and Algiers. It was essential that our senior Army, Navy and RAF officers conferred with the French authorities in these areas, or a meeting be held to cover all the areas which were under the control of the Germans at that time. All French Africa was under their control and some sort of concerted action must be agreed to before the Allies' invading forces landed, to avoid the French forces fighting against the Allies, with the Germans, in any surprise attack.

A British submarine with senior officers on board was sent from a port to land the negotiating officers at a pre-arranged point on the North African coast, where they were to proceed to a certain residence, some distance inland, to meet and put the residing French forces in the picture as to their intentions and strategy. A very clandestine operation and a very important one. Most dangerous, as German soldiers guarded the beaches with all manner of means to detect and stop intruders of any sort.

This story concerns one of my old shipmates, who was involved in the action. He was a petty officer telegraphist aboard the submarine which was to land the senior officers on the beach in North Africa, for the highly important conference with the French North African authorities.

The submarine arrived at the agreed point on the North African coast, she surfaced and after a cursory glance around the area, the inflatable dinghies were put over the side, the senior officers and aides got in, including my friend with his wireless set, and all were paddled ashore, disembarked, the dinghies were taken back to the submarines and she submerged. The officers and aides proceeded inland to the appointed rendezvous with the French.

My old shipmate settled on the beach, under cover, with his wireless set, in communication with the submarine; his main job was that when the senior officers returned he would call the sub on his wireless set, she would surface, send in the rubber dinghies, and bring everybody back to the submarine to leave for their base. All this was under the cover of darkness. Things were going well and my friend, complete with wireless set, sat on the beach not a worry in the world except keeping clear of the German patrols, when the hair on the back of his neck stood up. He heard a raucous growl just to one side of him. He looked in that direction and there stood a giant German shepherd dog. His ears were flat back, his teeth were showing, eyes glaring and he was 100% ready to attack.

My old shipmate realised at once that this was a real German Army guard dog. These dogs were allowed to roam the beaches, attack anyone they found, and make enough noise to attract the attention of the nearest German patrol. In his own words he said, 'I looked at this bloody menace and I did not know whether to go to the toilet or have a haircut.' He reached for his Service revolver and then thought, If I shoot it, the noise will attract the German Army. It was a calm quiet night, no wind and calm as a mill pond, any noise would carry for miles.

He thought, What the hell am I going to do? The whole success or failure of this expedition is now my responsibility.

Reaching for his revolver he had found a big handful of ship's Spratts dog biscuits in his jacket pocket, issued to Royal Navy personnel as hard tack emergency rations, which he had grabbed as he left the submarine. He pulled one out of his pocket and threw it carefully to the fearsome beast of a dog. The dog stopped growling and snarling, and happily chewed his biscuit, looking at my friend as much as to say, 'I can do with some more.' He kept breaking the biscuits in his pocket, and tossing bits to the dog to make them last longer as he did not know when the officers would return from their mission and he did not want to risk running out of biscuits.

It seemed an eternity before the senior officers and their aides returned to the beach; by this time the biscuits were getting a bit low.

One young officer returning to the beach saw the dog and almost shouted, 'A bloody German Army dog,' dragging his revolver from its holster.

A senior officer nearby said to him, in a loud clear voice, 'Put that bloody thing away do you want the whole German Army here?' (Exactly the sentiments of my old shipmate earlier.)

The senior officers then agreed, 'We can't shoot it. It is too well trained to allow somebody to knife or strangle it, any noise must be avoided. We must take it with us.' In the meantime, my friend had alerted the submarine, the rubber dinghies were soon on their way, the party was picked up (dog as well), and the submarine left and dived, to return to base, mission accomplished.

The submarine commander was very reluctant to allow the dog on board, but my friend had a word with him. (He was becoming attached to the dog and the dog to him.) He reminded the captain that he was leaving the sub at the end of the trip for shore duties (well-earned) and he would look out for, care for the canine monster. On the way back to base, when the submarine surfaced the dog went walkies on the upper deck and piddled against the periscope before going below again.

On arrival in port, the dog was taken over by my friend; he was absolutely devoted to him, they shared a shore billet together and lived happily for about two years. Life in the British Naval base at Alexandria passed quickly; doggie rations were a problem sometimes, but soon overcome by scheming sailors. During the two years he had the dog, on occasions he would go to the local hostelries and get a few jugs of beer, in the evenings, with the dog not far away, either walking in front of him, or just behind.

Alexandria was not a place to go out on your own in at night and return half-sozzled. Some of the local lads had a habit of nipping out of a dark alley, some two or three of them. You would be bowled over in two shakes, your wallet, Naval pay book identity card, and your shoes from your feet, would be gone with the villains.

During his two-year ownership of the dog, my friend didn't bother over this as his now faithful old friend would, coming up behind, attack the muggers before they knew where they were. On some two or three occasions he was under attack on his way back to base at night, and there would be an almighty roar and a black-brown flash would appear from nowhere. The dog bowled the assailants over, bit them everywhere he could and almost disrobed them; he would then give chase and happily return with lumps of clothing clamped in his huge jaws. These skirmishes made his day.

Like all good things, it had to end. My old shipmate was drafted to the United Kingdom for specialised duty, probably D-Day, and all his efforts to take his pal the dog with him were rejected. His only hope was to give him to the petty officer telegraphist who took over his job and his shore billet in Alexandria, who promised to look after him, rather than let him be destroyed.

On the day my friend had to leave for England he packed his gear in secret, shutting the old dog away during this. But the animal twigged something was going on. My old shipmate made a fuss of the dog, said his goodbyes and casually left the room as if he was going out somewhere, leaving him with his new owner. As he went down the stairs with his kit bag, the old dog went mad; he howled, barked, charged the door and tried to bite the handle off. With tears in his eyes my friend left the premises for the airport and home; he reckoned he had never felt so miserable in his life. Still he was comforted by the fact that he had done his best for the dog.

I often wonder after hearing this story if some German (Pongo) soldier ever wondered what happened to his pooch when it did not return to base after his patrol.

I Am Not Ready Yet

The year was 1941, and in the Greek area of the Mediterranean, around the Island of Crete a fierce battle raged between German and Allied Forces by land, sea and air, to seize and hold this strategic island. Our forces, Australian, New Zealand and British, were steadily overwhelmed by superior forces. Especially in the air, where Stuka dive bombers created havoc, our lads fought well but to no avail.

After many days of fighting, the Royal Navy had lost a lot of ships which we could ill afford to lose. At this time, an old shipmate of mine was serving in Lord Louis Mountbatten's destroyer flotilla in this battle. About half the flotilla of large, modern, well-equipped ships had been sunk by Stukas, including HMS *Kelly*, the flotilla leader, which was Lord Louis's command. Many of the sunken Royal Navy boats had survivors in the water, clinging to life-rafts covered in thick oil fuel, some wounded, when the gallant German Stuka and other pilots came down and machine gunned them and their rafts in the water, killing many who could have survived. This did not endear the enemy to the Royal Navy, who vowed vengeance, and got it in many ways.

My old shipmate's destroyer, which had been heavily involved in the battle, was ordered to withdraw from the area with what was left of the fleet, and proceed with them to Alexandria, the Egyptian Royal Naval base.

On receipt of the signal to withdraw, the Naval force proceeded to Alexandria and, when it was deemed safe, the weary gun crews, etc. who had had little sleep for days, and were low on ammunition, were ordered to stand down. They left their ack-ack and other guns to find somewhere to flop down and sleep. The ship, which had picked up many survivors from other sunken ships, was overcrowded. It was not easy to find a dry, warm spot to sleep. My old shipmate looked around in the twilight of the evening, along the ship's deck, and spotted feet sticking out from under the ship's torpedo tubes, above the warm engine room. He thought, Those crafty buggers know where to get. He wriggled under the torpedo tubes, with his coat rolled up for a makeshift pillow, elbowing his way in between them muttering, 'Move over you greedy baskets and let a tired gunner in.' He then fell into a sound sleep.

The following morning, a job was waiting that everybody tried to dodge: *burial party*. This involved the ship's sailmaker. (Yes, we had them in the modern Royal Navy for all canvas sewing jobs, smaller boats' sails, boat covers, screens, burials, etc.) The sailmaker, usually a petty officer, was accompanied by a few very reluctant heroes to assist him. Dead bodies from battles were placed on a canvas hammock. A heavy shell was placed at the feet of the corpse in order to take it to the bottom. The body and the shell were then enveloped in the canvas hammock. Starting at the feet, the ship's sailmaker sewed the corpse into the hammock from foot to head. On reaching the head, the last stitch, using a huge steel sailmaker's needle, was put through the nose of the corpse according to Naval tradition, to make sure the person was dead. The body was then ready for burial at sea by the padre.

On the early morning in question, the sailmaker and his helpers were on the deck of the destroyer, near the ship's torpedo tubes, to deal with all the dead bodies from the ship's crew, or those who had died after rescue, etc. These had all been put under the torpedo tubes for a couple of days during battle, until they could be dealt with for burial.

Hammocks were spread on deck, the bodies were dragged out from under the torpedo tubes by their ankles, and placed on them. One young, very reluctant hero grabbed a pair of ankles and dragged the body out from under the torpedo tubes onto a hammock. My old shipmate sat up and said to the reluctant hero in a loud voice, 'What the f— hell do you think you are doing?'

The reluctant hero let out a shriek and ran; he went round the ship's deck about three times before they caught him and treated him for shock. Yes, my old shipmate had picked a place to sleep among the gallant lads killed in action. (He had a hell of a job to live it down.)

Malta Convoy, June 1942

Under great secrecy, our destroyer sailed from Gibraltar; we knew there was 'something on' but did not know exactly what. We joined up with a convoy in the Mediterranean early in the morning which had just passed through the Straits of Gibraltar. There were a large number of warships surrounding six large, fast merchant ships, capable of a speed of fourteen knots. On joining the convoy, our captain told us, over the ship's loudspeakers, that we were to 'fight' this convoy through to Malta, or most of the way. Our hearts beat faster, as we had been on this 'run' for ages and we knew what the job entailed. We took station on the outer port destroyer screen, the 'hot seat' of the convoy, for a start.

We hoped that 'Jerry' would not detect us for some time, but we were disappointed. About 8 a.m. the next day, a bombing attack developed from a high level, another shortly after, and at about 10 a.m., one of the merchant ships was hit and disintegrated in a blinding flash; she was carrying ammunition, and there were only six survivors from this ship of some fifty crew members. We 'pressed on'.

Some time afterwards I decided I wanted to go to the lavatory and, as things were fairly quiet, I said to our officer in command of the gun battery (the ship's forward gun battery), 'I want to go to the toilet, will you hold the fort?'

I was a petty officer gunner captain of 'B' gun (the second gun in the battery from the front end of the destroyer). Lieutenant S, RNVR, a rather 'superior' individual who did not see eye to eye with me, due to his inexperience and complete lack of taking advice, no matter how tactfully offered, said, 'Carry On.'

I went below decks, got in the toilet, locked the door, sat down, then the alarm bells for 'action stations' sounded. I rushed back to my gun, an air attack developed, and we fired shell after shell and I did not get back to the lavatory. Between attacks I tried three times to get there, without success, and I knew that my gun crew (seven in number) must have been getting anxious for a visit to the toilet too.

I decided it was a waste of time getting to the lavatory under attack so I went below, partly filled a large iron pail with water and disinfectant, grabbed some spare toilet paper and went back to my gun deck. At the front end of the deck was a canvas shelter over an iron frame, used as a weather shelter in bad weather for the gun crew. I put the pail and disinfectant in the shelter, closed the front flaps and said to my gun crew, 'I use the pail first and then you can all take turns.' (I had asked Lieutenant S if he wanted to go first, and he said, 'No.') This was done and the only one on the gun deck who had not used the pail was Lieutenant S. (I think he was under the impression that he was an extraordinary being, different from everybody else. But he found he was not.)

During a lull in the battle, rather apologetically Lieutenant S said, 'I will use the lavatory, take over, Smithy.' I was second in command.

I replied, 'Yes, sir.'

He went into the shelter and he had no sooner 'got settled' on the pail than the bridge look-out's cry went up, 'Aircraft port.'

I looked to the port side and saw seven Sovoia Marchetti, Italian bombers, flying wave-high, 'wing-tip to wing-tip', coming in to attack the carrier. These planes carried two torpedoes each and could be dangerous.

By this time we were carrying out duty as 'torpedo buffer' to the aircraft carrier HMS *Eagle*. It was our duty as torpedo buffer to try to shield the aircraft carrier and get between any torpedo dropped and the aircraft carrier, to be hit by the 'tin fish', before it hit the carrier. The theory was that an older destroyer with one hundred and fifty men was more expendable than an aircraft carrier with one thousand five hundred men and vital fighter planes.

The torpedo bombers came in and pressed home their attack most vigorously; I gave the orders to bring my 4.7-inch gun battery into action. The ships and fleet guns 'crashed out', the Italian torpedo bombers went down one after the other, but one most courageously pressed home his attack on the carrier, HMS *Eagle*; we fired as fast as we could.

The Italian torpedo bomber was heading straight for us, we were between it and the aircraft carrier. It was several hundred yards away, I could see the markings on its wings vividly, bunches of sticks with a 'chopper' (axe) sticking out of both sides, the Italian emblem. Suddenly, it seemed, my gun fired, the Italian plane looked as if it had hit a brick as our 4.7 shell exploded on its snout. The plane 'staggered', went into a steep dive towards the *Eagle* and as it passed over us the gallant pilot released his torpedoes in a vain attempt to hit the carrier, however, his dive was too steep and the torpedoes would have hit the seabed before doing any damage. As the Italian plane was going down between my destroyer and the carrier I heard the staccato chatter of the 'Chicago piano' (eight-barrelled two-pounder Pom Pom AA gun) which was between HMS *Eagle*'s funnels, and saw the Italian plane blown to smithereens before it hit the water.

The captain of HMS *Eagle* signalled to us by Aldis lamp, 'Thank you for that. He was yours, he was a dead duck before my pom-poms got him.'

Whilst the attack was going on we had forgotten about Lieutenant S in our home-made toilet. During the attack, the 4.7-inch gun barrel, at a low angle, shooting at low flying torpedo bombers, went over the canvas shelter Lieutenant S was in, whilst firing.

When the attack was over, we heard plaintive cries for help from the shelter which had been split by blast from the gun, from front to rear. Lieutenant S RNVR, who had been blown off the pail, crawled out, 'covered in violets' from head to foot, swearing that I had been the cause of his disaster on purpose, despite the gravity of the situation. The laughter that followed was indescribable and he got madder than ever. He left the gun deck to change his uniform and bath. The convoy was attacked all day.

We eventually arrived at the Gibraltar end of the Straits of Messina, the 'E' boat alley of the Mediterranean. The larger ships withdrew from this convoy, covered by the older destroyers, at dusk and the ships most capable of the task went on, with what was left of the convoy, into the 'Valley of Death'. Big ships would be lost easily if they had tried to go on, and the war was at a crucial stage for warships.

We withdrew along the Mediterranean towards Gibraltar with the flagship and carriers intact. We all prayed for our shipmates who had gone on, knowing they were to have a dangerous, sleepless, battered night, 'without a hope in hell'.

The next morning at dawn we were all awake and round our ship's loudspeakers and the wireless office for news. The first was that the remains of the convoy was in sight of Malta but not within range of her shore batteries; most of the convoy was lost and some of the escorts. Spitfires from Malta were overhead and so was 'Jerry' from Sicily and Italy. About one and a half merchant ships were left, the 'half-ship' was the oil tanker *Kentucky* which had been blown in two but was still afloat. The vital aviation petrol still on board *had* to be got into Malta by hook or by crook – this was vital for the defence of the island. The tales of heroism on this day are far too numerous to mention, but this was the usual story of the Royal Navy and Merchant Navy since time immemorial.

To listen to the wireless message was like listening to an exciting football match; you willed, prayed, hoped for what was left of the convoy to get under the shelter of Maltese guns with its thin escort. Suddenly events took a dramatic turn. This part of the story, as far as I am concerned, was one of the most heroic actions of the war and as far as I know has never been fully published, or told. Why? I do not know. As I listened to the wireless messages, my heart filled with pride, that these men, the true 'bulldog breed' were of my generation and many were my friends.

A message was received from the senior officer of the convoy escort: 'Large force of Italian warships bearing down on convoy, consisting of battleships, heavy cruisers, light cruisers and destroyers.' Our hearts sank, as we had the only ships with guns capable of dealing with this force, and we were too far away to help in time.

The next signal was 'I am despatching HMS —, a Tribal Class destroyer, and HMS —, a P Class destroyer, to deal with this attack.' The two destroyers were the heaviest armed available with the convoy escort, their main attack weapons were eight torpedoes each, *but* it was like sending two Jack Russell terriers to sort out ten or twelve bull mastiffs. (Despite the Italians' reputation.)

The two destroyers steamed straight in at the Italian Fleet at high speed with explosive shells from the Italian heavy ships landing all round them, which out-ranged the destroyers' smaller guns. When at close range they fired two torpedoes each at the Italians and as soon as the splash of the 'tin fish' was seen by the Italians, they turned away from the convoy. The two destroyers followed up, firing all their guns, and when the Italian Fleet turned back again, they closed in and fired two more torpedoes each. The Italians turned away again, followed by the two British destroyers. These tactics were carried out until no torpedoes were left and, like a good night out with your girlfriend, it all had to end.

The convoy by this time was safe under the Maltese shore batteries, but the two attacking destroyers were in dead trouble. The Tribal Class destroyer was hit by an Italian eight-inch shell in her engine room and, naturally, stopped. The other destroyer, HMS *P*, under heavy Italian shell fire, went alongside the Tribal Class boat and passed her a tow line. They then set off for Malta, one towing the other, under heavy fire from the Italians.

HMS *P* then had a 'near miss' from a heavy shell which jammed her rudder hard over, and she could not steer.

The Tribal Class destroyer captain then ordered the captain of HMS *P* to 'slip the tow' and make his escape, steering by her main engines, not an easy task, but possible.

The captain of HMS *P* protested by signal, but had 'rank pulled on him'. He was obliged under threat of court martial to 'slip the tow' and make good his escape.

The Tribal Class destroyer stopped and, wallowing with no engines, then took on the Italian Fleet; she was a sitting duck until she was sunk, there was no surrender. What was left of her crew was captured and taken to a prisoner of war camp in Italy.

(Some of this story I obtained from old shipmates, who eventually returned to this country, who were survivors of the Tribal Class destroyer.)

One quirk of this magnificent story of Naval action was that the gallant captain of the Tribal Class destroyer, who survived this action, after saving what was left of the Malta convoy, was I understand killed in a British bombing raid in a prisoner of war camp in Germany (Hamburg) to where he had been transferred after the fall of Italy, some weeks before the war ended.

Will it ever be known if these two British destroyers, who were sent on a hopeless task, a virtual kamikaze mission, saved the remains of the vital convoy? What would have happened if they had failed or faltered, would Malta, then in a bad way, have had to surrender, depriving us of a vital base for the 'jump off' at Sicily and Italy?

I would submit that some gallantry medals were not awarded here that should have been. Why has this heroic action been kept quiet?

Memories

During the Second World War, on long convoy escort duties by the Royal Navy, hours were spent by the duty gun crews, huddled in damp, wet conditions near their guns ready to go into action at a moment's notice, their only shelter being a canvas shelter stretched over an iron frame. This was useless really against the biting cold, icy rain, and one was damp from the rear upwards. Huddled together for hours on end, some seven or eight of you in the canvas shelter only increased the temperature a little, but it was the best you could do.

In these four-hour watches, cold, wet, miserable, the only way to pass the time was to entertain each other with stories of your experiences in days gone by – days which were not very long ago for a group of young sailors; some were called up for the war, the others were regulars. Not many of them were left towards 1941/42, the time of this story.

We all took it in turns to tell a little story of our experiences to pass the time away. (No fairy tales, personal experiences only. If you gave a load of hogwash you were howled down and the next man on the rota took over.)

It became the turn of a good-looking able seaman in the gun crew. He was between twenty-two and twenty-four and he looked like an ancient Greek God; we knew of his physical prowess as we had seen him run, jump, tumble, leap etc. He was usually very reticent about himself but on the night in question, in the wet gun shelter, he seemed to unburden himself.

He explained that in 1937/38 he was at a public school in England. He was a top-class athlete and his speciality as a runner was the two hundred and twenty yards. He was picked to run for England at this distance in a large German city. He went to Germany with the England squad and, on arrival at the city, the squad were taken to the mountains outside the city to help them prepare for the very important events. (Germany was hell-bent on showing that their athletes were far superior to the rest of the world.) He went on to say that the England squad arrived at the mountain camp outside the city, which was snowbound, late at night, tumbled into their bunks in the cold wooden chalets and were soon asleep after travelling all day.

At some unearthly hour, about 5.30 or 6 a.m., they awoke to shouts of delight. He said, 'We wondered who was jumping about outside in the snow at that time in the morning.' They peered out of the frost-bound windows after scraping them and there were the German male and female athletes running up and down in the snow doing exercises, the men with only leather shorts on. They thought to themselves, These cranky bastards are trying to commit suicide, but they got the message – the German athletes wanted them out in the snow half-naked, or to lose face.

Our lads and lasses went out and joined them, fearing pneumonia, rolling in the snow half-naked and running, which calmed down the feeling of supremacy among the Germans. Cut short of their feelings of greatness, the German Games went on. Our narrator entered the stadium in the afternoon (nearly complete with frostbite from his rolls in the snow), lined up for the two hundred and twenty yard race and won it quite comfortably. A beautiful, blonde, blue-eyed German girl with long flaxen hair in braids came up to him as he stood on the winners' podium after the race, and crowned him with the winner's wreath of laurel leaves. When he stepped down from the podium after the ceremony, the girl was waiting for him. He had no more races. She said to him in perfect English, 'I am now your escort for the day. I will show you the city, take you wherever you want to go and then tonight after dinner and dancing at the best hotel in the city, you must come to bed with me and give me a baby, in the hotel.'

The cold, wet gun crew in the gun shelter suddenly came to life hearing this; they were all ears and various questions were fired at the athlete, some of which are not printable. He went on to explain that he said to the girl, 'Look here, old girl, I haven't been involved in this sort of thing before, is it really necessary that I come to bed with you?'

Amidst howls of disbelief from his fellow members of the gun crew (including me) he told us how he tried to dissuade her. She went on to explain that she was a top-class German two hundred and twenty yard event runner, and she had been ordered by the German authorities to keep close to the winner of the international event at two hundred and twenty yards and to keep with him and mate with him to try to produce a German top-class athlete at two hundred and twenty yards, male or female. She tearfully explained that if she returned to base and was not in the family way by him, she and her family would be in dire trouble.

We all pressed him as to 'When did you become a daddy?'

Like a true gentleman of pre-war days, he replied, 'You have heard the story, you work it out.'

No amount of ribbing or surmising would make him say any more.

Child Care Royal Navy Style

It was January 24, 1939, and the Royal Naval light cruiser of the South America–West Indies Squadron I was serving in was on a courtesy visit to Valparaiso, the Chilean city. We were lying in dock in the harbour – it was about 11 p.m. The sea was like a sheet of glass. The ship was tied up securely at both ends, bow and stern moorings.

Suddenly the ship started to shake and shudder, and various utensils, cups, saucers, and plates fell out of their racks and cupboards, some smashed. We looked out of the ship's portholes and saw the tall buildings on the dockside swaying from side to side. We wondered what on earth was happening. The incident lasted about a minute and then peace, calm, returned. Everybody was speculating as to what had happened and where.

It was not long before we found out. A message was received from the admiralty that a serious earthquake had occurred some two hundred miles south of Valparaiso, and the city of Conception, about the second largest in Chile, had been devastated. We were ordered with our chummy ship of the squadron lying nearby to proceed at full speed to the Chilean Naval base at Talcahuano, which I had visited some two weeks before to render what aid we could. We left Valparaiso together at high speed and later that day arrived at the Chilean Naval base.

We soon learned that the city of Conception had been virtually wiped out, with thousands of dead, ten miles away. Working parties of our ships' crews went up to Conception and were soon working on collapsed buildings, recovering bodies etc. No roads were available, no vehicles could help, everything had to be done by hand, and carried on foot. The ships' crews recovered some six hundred bodies for one mass grave and then eight hundred for another. It was estimated that the population of fifty-eight thousand had been wiped out in fifty-eight to fifty-nine seconds.

After four to five days the health hazard became acute, and orders were given to evacuate the city in order to avoid typhoid; the wrecked city was sprayed with quicklime when ready, by aircraft. Our chummy ship had left some two days before with eight hundred refugees for Valparaiso, and returned to collect some more. She re-loaded with eight hundred more and we took six hundred and left for Valparaiso together. You can imagine the problems on the ships with food, toilets, washing, especially as some of these refugees had had nothing since the earthquake except a handful of this and that from Conception to Talcahuano, some seven to ten miles away. The refugees were most grateful for the limited help we could give them and despite the language difficulties showed it. It was fortunate that the distance we had to carry them, two hundred miles, was not too far in fast warships in those days. (They cannot go any faster today.)

We had just left Talcahuano *en route* for Valparaiso, when three or four of us eighteen-year-old seamen were summoned to the gunroom. (This was the midshipmen's mess; budding Naval officers, they had been temporarily cleared out.) On the settee-type cushions (leather) round the room were some eleven orphan babies from three to four months to eleven months old. A mixture of boys and girls. An NCO said, 'Right you lot. You are now in charge of this lot,' grinning at his rhyming effort. 'Woe betide you if anything goes wrong on the trip, now watch it. I will have your guts for garters if there is a balls-up of any description.'

He then left. We looked at each other in dismay. What the hell did four eighteen-year-old lads from small families know about young babies? However, in true Naval tradition, we had a go.

Towels were pressed into service, cut up to make nappies. The only argument then was who was going to change the soiled ones on the babies yelling their heads off in dirty nappies. Here they were with a load of strangers, as hungry as hunters and we with no milk or feeding bottles; the din was deafening. The two lads who lost the toss for nappy changing went to work. It was a miracle the babies didn't get harpooned with our sick bay safety pins, but they managed. The other two young sailors went in search of baby food and utensils.

A call at the ship's sick bay resulted in three small bottles being collected just fit for the babies. We also cadged a pair of rubber surgical gloves. We cut off the fingers made holes in the ends and fitted them on the bottle necks, the nearest we could get to a baby's bottle. 'Now what about milk,' we thought. The ship's milk supply was evaporated Carnation tinned milk, clearly marked in capital letters 'UNFIT FOR BABIES'. As we had consumed gallons of the stuff in tea and it had never harmed us, we thought this had to be it.

We warmed the bottles in the galley (cookhouse) with diluted Carnation milk and returned to the 'field of battle'.

On arrival, the three bottles we had were given to three babies, who appeared to be most in need; this was followed by screams, yells and howls from the other eight who wanted to know where theirs was. Taking the bottles from the quiet feeders and giving them to the screamers did not help, it got worse. Plus there was an argument as to who was going to deal with the soiled nappies (handwashing only available); this was not helped by the fact that the ones who had had their nappies changed needed them changed again. Chaos reigned supreme, but help was at hand from an unexpected quarter. In the mayhem we had noticed that some Chilean refugee ladies on deck, young to middle-aged, had been watching our efforts through the large skylight above the gunroom for a while, and to them it was a sort of comic relief, in the middle of their troubles, they were almost rolled up with laughter at times.

They must have realised we were almost devoid of ideas, but had done no harm, and suddenly three or four of the ladies came into the gunroom smiling, shook hands and ushered us out. We could not speak the language, but we got the message we were to leave, they would take over. We left, but stayed and listened outside as the yelling, howling and general chaos subsided after about five to ten minutes and all was quiet and serene. We looked through the skylight into the gunroom, all the infants were quiet and looking at the ladies with adoring eyes as they moved around among them, touching and talking. Were we glad to get shot of that little lot? A few hours later we arrived in Valparaiso. The quayside, as we unloaded, was crowded with people, vehicles, ambulances, first aid vehicles, and food and drink stalls for the refugees' refreshment; it was a wonderful sight.

We saw the eleven 'mighty atoms' unloaded and put into vehicles. We thanked our lucky stars it was all over, as our period of domesticity with the babies had been enough, and we were eternally thankful to the ladies who took over.

A Policeman's Lot Is Not A Happy One

In the rural Suffolk Force I served in from about 1950–60, in each police division, of which there were three, we took it in turns to provide a night crime car. The car was sent for a seven-night stint from each divisional headquarters with a three-man crew: the driver from each divisional headquarters and two rural beat constables picked up at the start of the patrol from rural beat stations. The job of the car crew was to patrol the county on a pre-arranged route, checking churches for thieves nicking lead off the roofs, looking out for chicken and turkey rustlers (especially near Christmas), and sheep, cattle and pig rustlers. Also road checks were set up at intervals in various places to check occupants, cargo, destination etc. of any moving vehicle.

At the time of this story, the force vehicles had been at long last equipped with wireless receivers and transmitters, which had been available in bigger forces for ages, but due to economy the smaller forces had been forbidden to have them.

The night crime car with two younger constables as crew drew up at the local rural police station to collect the senior constable who would be in charge of the crew and the vehicle for the night. It was about 10.30 p.m. and the senior constable emerged from his station, all twenty stone of him, a giant of a man, complete with full uniform, helmet, greatcoat, cape and a bag containing food and drink to last the night. (It was enough to last a normal person a fortnight.)

He approached the car, a Hillman Minx, and made sure the junior constables (who had completed between six and ten years' service) were in the front seat, to use the wireless and write up the vehicle log. (A tedious task, as you logged everything you did, where you went, time, what you found and when you left the premises etc.) All this was out of the scope of the senior constable, a man of twenty years' plus service, who depended on his juniors to do all the spadework. He heaved his huge bulk into the back seat with difficulty, told his young men to follow the route etc., laid down by divisional headquarters (details of which were in the car) and then nodded off in the back seat, his usual routine on night car patrol.

The night was uneventful, and the only time they woke the man in charge was to have his refreshments at divisional headquarters. On return to the car he stretched out again in the back seat and nodded off. The crew proceeded on their routine.

At about 1.30 a.m. in a remote rural area, the vehicle wireless broke into life, 'Accident, slight injuries, — crossroads, can you attend? Two cars involved.'

The junior police constables replied to the effect they could and turned towards the scene of the incident some two or three miles away. As they got to the accident they woke the senior constable and informed him of the accident. He, rather disgruntled at his slumbers being disturbed, grunted, 'Get on with it. You know what to do.'

It was a freezing November night, hoar frost forming on hedges, and there was a slight fog. The two drivers in the accident and their passengers were already freezing cold, and when a nearby friendly farmer came out of his remote farmhouse about two hundred yards away and asked them to go into his house to make statements etc. to the police regarding the accident, they accepted his invitation. As the junior constables went to the house to make out their accident forms they went to the police vehicle and told the slumbering senior constable where they were going and why. He irritably said something like, 'All right, bloody well get on with it, don't disturb me.'

In the farmer's house they took statements, details of drivers etc. and had a hot drink with the farmer and car occupants; about one and a half hours elapsed. At the end of this time, the senior constable in the car must have been getting cold as, the car being stationary, the heater was not on. He heaved his twenty-stone-plus bulk out of the car, buttoned up his huge greatcoat, looked round and having spotted the light of the house he lumbered off towards them, muttering something like, 'What are those young sods up to, they are a long time?'

He made his way across open ground in the dark, with his torch; it was rough, overgrown, and a real mess. As he neared the house some fifty yards away he put his great size twelve–fourteen boot down on what he thought was garden, and then calamity. There was a loud noise of splintering rotten timber, he clutched at the air, which of course was a waste of time and went straight down through the rotten lid of the farm cesspit. This pit was full, due shortly to be emptied, some ten feet square and numerous feet deep, full of beautiful, smelly, squelchy human manure. Sloppy, wet – freezing cold.

He went in up to his shoulders, clutching the rotten wood surround of the lid of the cesspit with his fingers.

With his heavy police uniform his truncheon, handcuffs, books, boots, greatcoat, the weight was too much. Despite his great strength, with that lot pulling him down he could not hope to hoist himself out. The air was freezing and foggy, the house some fifty yards away, windows closed, curtains drawn, people talking inside. He was in what we in Suffolk call, a muddle.

He clung on with his fingers to the edge of the cesspit, hoisting himself now and again and yelling 'Help!' at the top of his voice. His wet attire, the freezing cold, his weight were all against him. He only just kept his mouth and nose above the stinking quagmire he was in and wondered how long it would be before he went under the mess.

By sheer luck, the junior constables finished their duties in the house and came out of the front door with the accident victims, to go back to the cars. Suddenly they all heard a plaintive 'Help!' from the garden. The two junior police constables rushed towards the noise, torches on, and came across the senior constable on his last legs with his mouth and nose nearly in the juice. They grabbed his shoulders and gave a heave. He hardly moved except to get his nose and mouth a little higher from the manure. The farmer and others quickly arrived, the farmer got a rope, it was secured to the upper part of the victim and they all pulled on the rope until they had the senior constable on firm ground near the pit, like a stranded whale covered in 'chocolate'. The smell was diabolical, and the people all shied away from him. After a few minutes he recovered his composure. He was not injured, and the various people left. The senior constable stood up after a while, frozen, wet through and not very happy. He said, 'Get me home as soon as you can.' It was 3.30 a.m., some four miles from his home station (lucky for him it wasn't further), freezing and foggy. He moved towards the car.

One of the junior constables who was the driver said, 'Hang on, old man, this is a new car, you cannot get in that covered in liquid manure from head to foot.' He quickly surveyed the situation and said, 'The only way we can get you home is if you stand on the rear bumper, lie across the sloping back of the car and hang on to the roof guttering with your fingers.'

The now desperate man would agree to anything, so he clambered on to the back of the new car, and clung on with his already freezing fingers for dear life. The driver then drove at about five–ten miles per hour through freezing fog to his station about four miles away. On arrival, the two junior constables prised the senior constable off the back of the car and were helping him up his driveway when the bedroom window shot up and an irate female shouted, 'Who is that?' Her husband, the senior constable, was home early, and she wanted to know why.

He called to her, 'It is all right, dear, I had to come home early as I fell in a cesspit.'

She shouted back, 'Don't you come into the house like that, strip off on the front lawn, removing everything.' She then added, 'I will run you a bath.'

The junior constables helped him to strip down to his birthday suit on the front lawn, surrounded by hoar frost, freezing fog etc. They then delivered his near-naked body to his wife in the house who took him to the bathroom, and a hot bath. A senior officer called at his station the following day to view his damaged, manure-soaked uniform, boots, etc. and supervised the starting of a bonfire and burning of the lot, before his uniform was replaced. Fortunately the gentleman in question suffered no after effects *but* if you saw him on duty after this incident and asked him when he would do it again so you could come and watch, he got a little bit agitated and you had to depart quickly to avoid a large police boot.

Do You Know He Is Scottish?

In about 1952, on the outskirts of a Suffolk market town, one of the local constabulary was on patrol at about 2.30 p.m.; pub closing time was then about 2 p.m. As the officer approached a parked car on the road with the bonnet lid up, a gentleman was bending over the engine, giving it some attention. As the officer approached the vehicle, the driver was looking under the bonnet. The officer stopped and saw that the man was trying to resuscitate the engine. He was blowing down the electrical plug leads, in turn. The constable said to the driver, 'Are you having some trouble?'

To which the man replied, 'Yes, I am trying to clear a petrol blockage.' His voice was slurred and the officer noticed that when he stood up to speak to him he had to hold on to the vehicle to avoid falling over.

He said to him, 'Is this your car, sir?'

The driver said, 'Yes, of course it is.'

He said, 'You are driving?'

The man replied irritably, 'Why do you ask me all these questions? Of course I am the driver.'

The officer replied, 'It appears to me that you have been drinking and are not fit to be in charge of a motor vehicle etc.' He then arrested the man, cautioned him, got him to the nearest telephone and requested transport for a drunken driver. (No walkie-talkies in those days. Necessity was the mother of invention.)

After a wait a police car arrived, and the officer and his prisoner left for the station. On arrival he was seen by a doctor, put through various tests by him and was certified by the doctor as drunk. He was put in cells and, when sober, released on bail. He collected his car, which had been brought to the station after his arrest, and left.

On his next appearance at the local magistrates court the driver entered a plea of Not Guilty, with a solicitor, and asked for trial by jury at the next county quarter sessions. Everybody in legal circles, including police, thought he must be crazy. In those good old days the usual penalty was £25 fine, licence endorsed, plus maybe a few weeks disqualification, if you were unlucky in the magistrates court. *But* in a lot of cases the legal profession pulled so many smart alec tricks to get clients acquitted that the whole thing became a farce. When the Government acted in came the breathalyser etc., this helped to curb the legal profession's activities.

The gentleman in question, after preliminary hearings, was arraigned before the local county quarter sessional court and pleaded Not Guilty.

The prosecution's counsel called his evidence, including doctor, witness etc. and the arresting officer, immaculate in his best uniform, medal ribbons etc. on his left breast, gave his evidence. The prosecution case was almost finished, and the arresting officer was the last to be cross-examined by a fresh-faced young counsel for the defence. (In those days the defence had only to attack the doctor, and the main police evidence, create a doubt in the jury's mind, men who also drunk fifteen pints of beer before driving their car and were all right, and the case was home and dried for a Not Guilty verdict.

The young counsel tried to twist, alter and misinterpret the doctor's evidence without much success. Now came the turn of the burly arresting officer, erect in the witness box. The defence counsel checked with him from his initial evidence-in-chief, the time, date, place of the incident, what he saw, what he heard, what he did, with questions to verify his original evidence all the way along. The young defence counsel was feeling that he had got the police constable on the ropes ready for the knockout, despite his lack of apparent success in his cross-examination.

He adopted a fighting pose of thumbs in his armpits stance, and said to the police constable, 'You stated in your examination-in-chief that when you approached my client on the road, attending to his car, he answered your questions and his speech was slurred, what do you mean by that?'

The officer replied, 'I could hardly understand what he was saying.'

The young counsel asked, 'Why was that?'

He replied, 'He was drunk and couldn't speak properly.'

Counsel then said, 'I do not think this is the answer; I put it to you that you just could not understand his accent.'

The officer became silent and the young counsel, sensing he had got him groggy verbally, looked round the court at the audience and, oozing with confidence, said to the constable, 'Are you aware, Officer, that this man is a Scot, and the reason you thought his speech was slurred was that he spoke in his Scottish brogue, which you do not understand?'

The constable, without batting an eyelid, said, 'No, sir, that is not the case.'

Counsel, puffing himself with success, looked round the court again and said, 'So you are conversant with the Scottish language, brogue etc., Officer'?'

The officer did not reply. Goaded on by his seeming success, the defence counsel said (addressing the court), 'It appears we have with us today an expert on the Scottish language, the brogue etc. Will you now tell the court where you gained your expertise in the Scottish language?' The officer still remained silent. Counsel, again lulled into a sense of false security, then said, 'Come along, Officer, the court is waiting for an answer, where did you get your expertise?'

After another slight pause, the officer looked at the young counsel and court and said, 'During the last war, sir, I was a regimental sergeant major in the 51st Highland Division from early in the war in the Western Desert, Al Alamein etc. to Italy, D-Day, the Normandy Landings, Caen, and up to the German Army surrender at Luneberg Heath. During this four to five year period I dealt with, and spoke to a large number of Scottish soldiers and I think I know enough now to understand their language, brogue etc.'

The young counsel for the defence looked as if somebody had clouted him on the head with a baseball bat; his jaw dropped. There was a distinct silence in the courtroom for a few minutes, and counsel just managed to address the court. 'That is the case for the defence,' he said as he sat down. (He had no other witnesses and it was evident he did not or dare not call his Scottish client to give evidence.)

He was completely shattered. The jury retired and shortly returned with a Guilty verdict. The Scottish gentleman driver was disqualified for one and a half years from driving, fined £150, licence endorsed. (I think afterwards he wished he had put his hands up in the magistrates court.)

After the hearing at the quarter sessions, the police officer who had been involved in the case was waiting in the corridor of the court, for another police case, when the young counsel in the drunk in charge case breezed into the court corridor came to the officer concerned and shook hands with him. He said, 'Well done, officer. That has taught me a lesson I shall always remember. I stuck my neck out in there and I got one of the biggest kicks up the a— I shall never forget.' He then left.

False Teeth

Shortly after World War II a young man of some twenty-two years joined the Suffolk Constabulary and after his initial training was posted to a large east coast town where he would do his initial training at outside police duties. After a couple of months of duty, he was on an afternoon shift of 2–10 p.m., and an elderly sergeant was on duty with him.

The experienced sergeant had noticed the young man was rather apprehensive about blood, injuries, anything physical etc. and decided he had got to get used to this or leave the job. He had had a talk with him and given advice, to no avail it seemed.

On the afternoon in question, in the town mortuary nearby was a body, a road accident victim. The sergeant had nipped round to the mortuary, unlocked it, went in and cleaned the mortuary slab with disinfectant, removed his own false teeth, wrapped them in a white, disinfected cloth, and laid them on the slab next to the head of the body.

He then returned to the station where he knew the new recruit would be. He said to him, 'Have you seen a dead body yet, old son?'

The lad replied, 'No.'

The sergeant said, 'You will have to get used to this, ready for when you attend a post mortem examination with the pathologist; this is worse.'

The young constable nodded.

The sergeant said, 'Right, there is a body in the mortuary, come with me and you can view it.'

The constable followed the sergeant to the mortuary and they unlocked the door and entered. The body was lying covered with a sheet on the mortuary slab. The sergeant said, 'I will remove the sheet and you can look.' He did this and the constable did not look very happy at the sight of a body.

As he removed the sheet, the sergeant said to the constable, 'What is this here?' He pointed to the wrapped bundle of false teeth.

The shaken constable said, 'I don't know.'

The sergeant picked up the bundle and unwrapped it, revealing the false teeth. He said, 'My word, false teeth, just what I need, a new set.' He popped the teeth into his mouth, rattled them chomped on them and said, 'Just right, perfect fit, he won't need them any more.' (Indicating the corpse.)

The young constable tried to be sick, ran out of the mortuary and was far from happy when he found out what the sergeant had done as part of his initiation. (All part of the unofficial training programme.)

Loveable Lady Tramp

It was the early 1950s in a small Suffolk market town and I was a serving police officer of a few years' service, due to Armed Forces service prior to this. In the town lived a very industrious family well-respected by all. One of the family, however, was an offshoot, a bit of an embarrassment to the rest of the family; she chose to roam the countryside with all her possessions done up in cloth bundles. She sold matches, shoelaces, and other bits and pieces in the surrounding villages to eke out an existence and seemed to be quite happy providing she was outdoors and left alone.

Her family tried on many occasions to get her to come back home and live there but on entering the house she demanded all doors, all windows be opened wide, day and night, and would endure no heat of any description. Not wishing to get pneumonia, the family objected, so she always departed. She roamed the countryside in reasonable weather, and in the depths of winter she sought refuge in a local religious establishment in a village not far from the town, where the good nuns cared for her till she departed, mainly in the spring.

At the time of this story she was about sixty years of age. I was out in the town one day with my duty sergeant on foot patrol; we saw this good lady and she was having difficulty crossing the road, as traffic was a bit heavy. A passer-by got hold of her arm and offered to assist her across the road. She pulled away and the language she used to the good Samaritan made one blush. (Me, after sixteen years' Naval service.) The sergeant said to me as I went to intervene, 'Stay here. Keep well away from her and don't speak to her unless she comes to you. You have been warned she is a right b—. If you tangle with her, just let her go on her way, usually she is harmless unless provoked – then watch out.'

About this time the local 'tea leaves' (thieves) were stealing lead off all the local church roofs. The order had gone out to all foot patrols and mobile patrols, to pay attention to churches, day and night, to try to stop this particular crime.

One of the force's local, mobile patrols, a car and two officers, went to a village church not far from the town at about 1 a.m. They checked the church doors, windows and the vicinity for parked vehicles, and finally looked at the church porch seats at the main entrance. There in the pitch dark, asleep on her bundles of possessions, was the lady tramp. They both kept quiet, left the church porch and decided to play a prank on the good lady, still asleep. (Where she was doing no harm.) They both were aware of who she was and of her reputation for a fiery temper and obscene language.

They returned to the police vehicle and got from the boot a huge white dust sheet which, in those days, was used to cover police patrol cars when not in use in the garage. One officer hid behind the gravestones near the church porch, the other put the white dust sheet over his head, went into the porch with his torch on under the sheet and stood alongside the lady tramp, who was still sound asleep in the church porch.

He began to make moaning noises etc. and in a few minutes the lady tramp was awake. She let out a blood curdling shriek, leapt two or three feet in the air, still screaming, and dashed down the church path towards the road, waving her bundles in the air.

The chap behind the gravestones was laughing so loudly the lady heard him and came back. She was livid, and she ran at them with her bundles; they dodged her, got back to the car, still nearly in tears with laughter, jumped in and drove away, with the lady tramp kicking the back of the police car, and using language like an experienced Army regimental sergeant major. (Luckily there were no repercussions. When you think what could have gone wrong.)

Mistaken Identity

It was some twenty-five years ago and a magistrates court day and licensing sessions in a Suffolk town. All the licensing business was dealt with first. All the pub landlords etc. were there to apply for a licence to sell booze at village hall dances, fêtes, flower shows etc., places other than their licensed premises. All went according to plan till a pub landlord was called to apply for his licence. He had not yet arrived. As the landlord came from a village some ten miles from the town it was assumed that either his car had broken down or he had been involved in some other mishap, and the clerk of the court put the case to the end of the court list, and other court matters were dealt with.

The court, towards the end, was running late. The clerk of the court and magistrates wished to conclude the court business as quickly as possible. He consulted his list and the last case was a young eighteen-year-old girl seeking a paternity order for her baby boy from her boyfriend who admitted paternity but 'shied away' from marriage.

The clerk of the court called to the court usher to bring in the young lady seeking the paternity order. This was done and a beautiful, well-dressed girl was ushered into court, evidently rather embarrassed. The clerk of the court asked for her full name and address and asked whether she was seeking a paternity order against her boyfriend.

She replied, 'Yes.'

The clerk then said, 'I understand he admits being the father of your child and does not intend to dispute the facts.'

The girl replied, 'Yes that is correct.'

The clerk said to her, 'Is he present at this court today?'

She said, 'Yes, he is outside in the court corridor.'

The court clerk called to the court usher standing near the door.

'Call Mr — into court.'

The elderly retired police sergeant, now the court usher, was hard of hearing and could not hear the name, but he opened the door of the court, saw the only male person outside, grabbed his arm and said, 'Come with me, sir.' (He assumed this was the person required in court, but the father of the child had gone to the toilet a few minutes before he was called for court.)

The court usher delivered the man from the corridor, whom he had pulled into court, alongside the lovely blonde girl. The clerk of the court said to the man, 'The court is running late and I do not want to waste any time. Now, do you admit being the father of this young lady's child?'

The man, some thirty-five to forty years old, looked at the girl, went as red as a beetroot, his mouth was opening and closing like a goldfish in its bowl, and no sound came out; his eyes were bulging and everybody wondered what was the matter with him.

The clerk of the court looked at the prosecuting police inspector who was shaking his head from side to side and said, 'Is there something wrong, Inspector?'

To which he replied, 'Yes, sir, this man is the licensee of the — [naming the pub] – he is the one who was not here earlier to apply for his licence to sell intoxicating liquor at a dance in his village hall.'

The clerk of the court sent the licensee outside once again and told the court usher to bring in Mr —, the reluctant father, who was some twenty years old. He had now returned from the toilet and was brought into court by the court usher, and the paternity order was soon granted.

The licensee was granted his occasional licence, after apologising for being late. He was still in a state of shock as he left the court, as he was a happily married man.

Night Duty Thrills

In the early 1950s I was a serving police officer, on night duty shift (10 p.m. to 6 a.m.) in a small Suffolk market town. At about 2.30 a.m. I had just finished my refreshment break, tea and sandwiches in the police station, which was also a divisional headquarters in those days.

The duty sergeant said to me, 'You go out and take the town centre beat, check all the usual property. [Not a mammoth task.] I will see you at 4 a.m. at the telephone kiosk.'

I left the station muffled up in heavy uniform as it was a cold November morning, damp with fog and pitch black.

I walked up the main street – it was as quiet as the grave. No cars, no lorries, no people, no lights. It was a rural town off the main traffic routes. On the way up the street I went into shop doorways 'shaking hands' with door handles and pushing doors to ensure they were locked. All side and back doors and windows were also checked to see they were secure and that the burglars were not at work or had just left.

About 3 a.m. I was approaching the end of the main street; all was dark, cold, and quiet. About seventy-five yards away was a small yard light on a house which cast an eerie pale light in the mist and fog. I went into a shop doorway, checked the doors and windows and stepped out of the doorway onto the pavement, looking up the street in the direction I was going. I then stopped dead and froze where I stood, with the hair on my neck standing straight. (Despite being an ex-servicemen of sixteen years in the Royal Navy all over the world, and during World War Two.) I took a deep breath.

Coming towards me, on my side of the street, was a white shadowy figure, emitting a moaning noise, about thirty–forty yards away. I could see a human-like form, with arms and hands stretched out to full length in front. The head was held high and I could see it was something about five foot tall. As it came closer I could see a white, partially bald head with greyish-white hair at the back which was standing up straight like a lion's mane; it had bulging eyes, staring straight in front. I thought to myself, What the hell is it? A ghost, something from outer space? To put it mildly I was not very happy.

As the thing/person got nearer to me, by instinct I looked at the clothing. I shone my torch on it as it passed about a couple of yards away and saw the feet had plaid carpet slippers on, and the lower limbs had white long john underpants from ankles to waist with a white woollen long-sleeved vest, all as worn by elderly gentlemen. I heaved a big sigh of relief and went after the 'figure', now I knew it was an elderly man.

I walked beside him and said, 'Are you all right?'

He didn't falter, arms still outstretched. He said, 'It is those American planes up there [raising one arm to point upwards], every time they come over they stop my heart. I know they are trying to kill me.'

I now knew I had a mental person on my hands and, taking his arm, I said, 'Come on old chap you come with me.'

We walked to the police station about half a mile away. Nothing was said *en route*. I knew I had to get him in the warm quickly, on a freezing night with him in his underwear.

On entering the police station front door, I ushered 'my friend' inside into the charge room where the sergeant was having his tea and sandwiches. As he caught sight of my 'capture' his jaw dropped and then he almost choked on his sandwich, spitting it across the room (he was a long service police sergeant, an ex-guardsman, World War II etc.) He virtually shouted at me, 'Where the bloody hell did you find him?'

I said, 'Sergeant, I was in the main street, checking property, and I found him wandering in his undies and apparently in need of help, so I brought him in "for a warm" and to see if we could sort him out.'

The sergeant said, 'What is wrong with him?'

Tongue in cheek I said to my friend, 'Tell the sergeant what is wrong.'

With arms outstretched he looked really wild and launched into his explanation of 'American planes flying overhead and stopping his heart in an effort to kill him.'

The sergeant let out a muffled gurgle and said to me, 'Get him out of here and then you sort him out, you found him.'

I took him to another part of the police station found a wooden bench, blankets and a pillow near an open fire and got a colleague to watch him whilst I made further enquiries; 'the problem' was soon sound asleep.

Not long afterwards a telephone message was received from an anxious brother of the found man to the effect that his brother was 'on licence' with him from a local mental hospital. He had put him to bed, and went to sleep himself, earlier that morning, when he woke up at about 4.30 a.m. his brother had gone. He was most apprehensive regarding his brother as his house was only yards from the river, running through the town. He was assured his brother was okay and at the police station asleep. The brother told me who the local family doctor was and I phoned him and asked him to come and examine 'our friend'.

The doctor's reaction to my request was a bit out of the ordinary. His first question after I told him the details of finding his patient during the night, in his undies, wandering the street was, 'How are you feeling?'

I thought the doctor, a dour, very efficient Scotsman had flipped his lid. I replied, 'I am all right, what about the patient?'

He replied, 'That bloody man and his appearance frightens me to death in my surgery in broad daylight so how the hell you reacted in the dark, on your own, I will never know.'

He came and did his examination, the man was okay physically as apparently I had run across him on a cold freezing night a short time after he got out of his brother's house. The man, some seventy years of age, was returned to his local mental hospital the same day. (He was lucky, if he had wandered, in his clothing, at sub-zero temperatures for long, he would have been in a bad way or dead when found.)

Out of the Mouths of Babes

One day in the 1970s I was walking in the Suffolk village where I lived. As I reached the village green I saw a young local lad, some eight or ten years old, struggling to replace a rather black oily chain on his small bicycle, without success.

I went over to him and asked him if he wanted any help, to which he replied, 'Yes, please.'

He then said to me, 'Have you got a bicycle?'

I said, 'Yes.'

The boy said, 'Is it a new one?'

I replied, 'No, it is a very old one.' (I was at the same time thinking of the 1925 model 'sit up and beg' police-type Raleigh bicycle I had owned for some twenty years, which I had bought second-hand.)

The little lad looked at me with shining eyes and said, 'Does yours have one of those great big wheels at the front, and a little tiny wheel at the back?'

I said, 'No, son, not quite as old as that.'

He rode off.

On my way home, this encounter set me thinking; here was I in my fifties being asked by a youngster if my bicycle was a penny farthing. I thought I looked rather young for my age – now I had my doubts.

Pursuits of Love

In about 1964, in Newmarket, Suffolk, headquarters of racing, I was a serving police sergeant one day at around 1 a.m. on a Sunday, the usual fighting and the tumult had ceased from the usual Saturday night hubbub and a few of the night shift were having their meal break.

In the corner of the room the small telephone switchboard suddenly came to life with a 999 call. One of the lads leaned over from his chair and plugged in; we were all watching and listening, ready to go if necessary. The officer answering the call had a look of amazement on his face as he unplugged from the switchboard.

Somebody said, 'What was that all about?'

The recipient said, 'He must be an escaped mental patient. The deputy matron of the nurses' home across the road has just caught a lad who climbed into her bedroom window and tried to get into bed with her. She wants us to collect him.'

After the initial laughter and remarks two constables went to investigate. In the hallway of the nurses' home they met the large irate figure of the deputy matron in her night clothes, complete with hairnet and curlers. Under her arm she had a seventeen to eighteen-year-old stable lad/jockey type. The deputy matron demanded that the intruder be arrested and dealt with.

He was removed from the premises white-faced and shaking, although rather relieved to be out of the deputy matron's clutches, and brought to the police station. We realised that this badly shaken and terrified young man was no burglar or rapist.

He was given a cup of tea and allowed to recover and collect his wits. Then one of the arresting officers said to him, 'What has been going on tonight, you are in a bit of a predicament breaking into the nurses' home and trying to get into bed with the deputy matron.'

He went a shade of green and said, 'I will tell you.' He was still shaking.

He said, 'I went to the Saturday night dance in the Memorial Hall in the High Street. I had a few drinks and met this lovely Scandinavian nurse who works at the hospital. We danced and cuddled all evening when she suddenly said she had to be in the nurses' home by 11.15/11.30 p.m. and she must leave. She invited me to go back to the nurses' home when I left the dance, telling me how to get in the grounds, which side of the building to go to, and to count the ground-floor windows up to eleven or twelve. I would know which one as it would be opened at the bottom to let me in. I got there, counted the windows and saw one open at the bottom; I pushed it up, and climbed in. I saw the bed with a single figure in it and after getting ready I got into bed, as I thought, with my Scandinavian beauty.'

He then paused and said, 'The bedclothes flew back and this big Irish woman with curlers came at me shouting, 'What the hell do you think you are doing?' She grabbed me and I nearly fainted. You know the rest."

We checked his story with the blonde nurse (in the room next to the deputy matron), she confirmed his story and we let the lad go in time to get to work. He gladly went on his way.

Married Bliss

In the early 1970s at a Suffolk police divisional headquarters about 9.30 p.m. one night, a message was received in the control room from the local hospital to the effect that an elderly gentleman from one of the outlying rural villages some twelve miles away had died. This came with a request from the hospital for the police to inform his wife of his death, as she was not on the telephone. The hospital nurse who had telephoned was asked if the 'news was expected' by the wife, to prevent any unnecessary grief to the bereaved woman when passing on the message. The nurse said the deceased had been ill for a long time but the death was not really expected.

The duty inspector was wondering how to deliver the message when the constable in charge of that area unexpectedly called into divisional headquarters to collect papers, reports, etc. He was on his way back to his station to go off duty. The inspector called him into his office and told him the message, the address, name etc. and told him to call at the address on his way home and to be careful and as discreet as possible.

The constable, very senior in service, left the divisional headquarters to deliver the message. The next day he returned to work and the inspector asked him how he had got on with the delivery of the 'agony message'.

He replied, 'I got a bit of a surprise. I got to the house at about 11 p.m. and all was in darkness.'

He had knocked on the front door and after a few minutes the bedroom lights went on. The upstairs window was pushed up and a lady with curlers in her hair put her head out of the window.

She shouted at him, 'Who is that?'

He introduced himself and said, 'Are you Mrs —?'

To which she shouted, 'Yes, what do you want?'

He replied, 'I have a message for you about your husband in hospital?'

She replied, 'What is it?'

The officer kept his voice down and said, 'I am sorry, he has passed away.'

She yelled at the constable, 'Did you wake me up at 11 p.m. to tell me this? That old bugger should have been dead years ago.' And she then slammed the window shut.